366

Daily Bible Devotions for 10-16 year-olds

Mrs. Margaret Adegboyega

366 DAILY BIBLE DEVOTIONAL FOR 10-16 YEAR-OLDS

BY

MRS. MARGARET ADEGBOYEGA

Copyright 2016

ISBN 978-1530077892

Published in the United Kingdom

Cover Design and Page Layout
Kenteba Kreations
www.kentebakreations.com

All rights reserved. No portion of this book may be used without the written permission of the publisher, with the exception of brief excerpts in magazines, articles, reviews etc.
For further information or permission, address:

Mrs. Margaret Adegboyega
5a Priory Hill,
Dartford, Kent
DA1 2BD

E-mail: mobola.segun@yahoo.com

All scripture quotations are from the King James Version of the Bible except otherwise stated.

Foreword

Jesus was very much displeased when His disciples prevented the young ones from coming to Him.

In Mark 10:14,15 He said

> *'... Permit little children, and forbid them not, to come unto me; for of such is the kingdom of God. Verily I say unto you, whosoever shall not receive the kingdom of God as a little child ... shall not enter into it'.*

Then verse 16 follows on to say that Jesus '... took them up in his arms, put his hands upon them, and bless them'. This goes to show the kind of affection, value and loving passion that the Lord Jesus has for the young ones, particularly those who dare to follow Him.

Apostle Paul's admonition to young Timothy then was, and still is to the youths today

> *'Let no man despise thy youth, but be thou an example of the believers in word, in conduct, in love, in spirit, in faith, in purity'*
> *1 Timothy 4:12.*

This devotional, therefore, is primarily designed to help Christian youths maintain a regular and balanced Christian life. It is simple, straightforward, down to earth and user friendly. Each day starts with a casual greeting to God the Father, God the Son and God the Holy Spirit; presuming that devotion will be the first thing to be done at the waking up in the morning. It is then followed by a short reading passage, a watch word for quick meditation based on the passage and then a closing prayer, again based on the passage read.

I have known Margaret Adegboyega for about twenty years now. She is very much involved in the youth ministry; and very passionate too about the physical and spiritual well being of young people. It is often said that children are members of the Church of tomorrow. Margaret doesn't see it that way. Margaret's desire to see young people grow spiritually in their daily walk with God has led to the production of this devotional. I, therefore, pray that the Lord will use this devotional to enrich your spiritual life.

Apostle (Dr.) John Babatope Ameobi
Apostolic Church, Newcastle upon Tyne, UK

Preface

Greetings in the precious name of our Lord and Saviour Jesus Christ – Who is the keeper of our life, and through Whom we live, we move and have our being. My passion in life has been focused on seeing children grow up, train and equip them so as to enable them walk in ways pleasing to the Lord. More importantly in recent months, God has placed a burden on my heart to make this vision more articulate and clearer by means of a printed material.

The Holy Scripture says that in Psalm 127 verse 3 that "Children are the heritage of the Lord." Precisely, on the 26th April 2005 while teaching leaders in the children section of my local church, God laid it upon my heart to write a daily devotional for future pace-setters that will change the face of Christianity as we see it in modern times (Habakkuk 2:1-2).

It is at this moment that I have time to put in writing what the Holy Spirit told me, i.e. to write a devotional for the children in the western world because it is constantly changing and as Christians, we should grow in the Lord so that we are equipped with necessary spiritual wisdom to maintain our Christian distinctiveness, yet being attractive to the world around us. It is imperative that we constantly find new ways to make our relationship with God more appealing to younger individuals who think that what it involves in following Jesus is all cost and sacrifice without any gain – (1 Corinthians 2:9).

The giants inside our youths have to be nurtured to its full capacity and extent, in order to ensure that they reach their full potential. However, this cannot be done by sheer will power or mere motivation, but only by the Spirit of God working through human hearts – (Deuteronomy 29:29; Zechariah 4:6).

This devotional teaches children how to cultivate an intimate but also entertaining relationship with Jesus Christ, our Lord and Saviour. The simplicity in which it has been written makes it easy to read and understand. It only requires about 20 minutes of your time daily (probably in the morning before leaving home), and it will enable you to commune with the Holy Spirit of God so as to guide you in every aspect of your day. The Lord will make you a force to be reckoned with in Jesus name. Amen.

There are real proofs! For example, it can be seen in the lives of Daniel, Uzziah and David; all of whom started at a young age and eventually became men who loved and served God, and became elder statesmen in their generations. Moreover, because God is Yahweh: the same yesterday, today and forever, the same power that was evident in their lives can be evident in yours. You just have to be determined, purposeful, have a thirst and hunger for Christ Word, believe what you read and avoid distractions. That kind of discipline, dedication and devotion to God will eventually pave way for you to reach the top.

Prepare your heart, have a continuous thirst and positive expectations for the word that is coming to you each day from this devotional, and I can assure you that your future as a world changer will become a reality – (Proverbs 4:18).

I pray that the Holy Spirit will make your eyes of understanding to be enlightened in Jesus' name.
Amen.

Yours Sincerely in Christ Jesus,
Mrs. Margaret Adegboyega.

Confessions

If you have not at a time give your life to Lord Jesus or you wonder away and you come back to Jesus. You need rededication. So declare this confession before you start this book.

Father in the name of Jesus.
I know I am a sinner.
Thank you for finding me.
Today I believe with my heart that you died for me and confess with my mouth that you are my Lord and saviour.
Thank you for delivering me from the power of sin and Satan.
Now I am born again.
Amen.

January 1

Good morning Father, Good morning Jesus, Good morning Holy Spirit.

Reading Passage
Psalms 119:100-102

Find your watch Word
Psalms 119:105 (Memorise)

Prayer
Pray that the Holy Spirit teaches you today to restrain your feet and all your body from every evil way, for God has made you to understand more than the ancients.
It is the beginning of the year.
Pray that the Holy Spirit will protect you through the year from every evil. Amen.
May the Lord bless you in Jesus name!

January 2

Good morning Father, Good morning Jesus, Good morning Holy Spirit.

Reading Passage
Psalms 92:1-5

Find your watch Word
Psalms 92:10 (Memorise)

Prayer
Give thanks to the Lord today for His mercies endure forever.
Sing all types of songs to thank and praise God. You need to dance if you will, for His faithfulness every day and night.
Say "Your truth shall be my shield and my buckler".
Thank Him for He will exalt your horn and anoint you with fresh oil. Give thanks, give thanks, and give thanks. Amen.
May the Lord bless you in Jesus name!

January 3

Good morning Father, Good morning Jesus, Good morning Holy Spirit.

Reading Passage
Hebrews 2: 1-4

Find your watch Word
Hebrews 4:12 (Memorise)

Prayer
The word of God is powerful; it is a weapon against any affliction you are facing at this moment.
Remember God's word to Joshua in Joshua 1:8 (This book of the law shall not depart from thy mouth...).
This is a command to speak God's word always. So speak the word of God to your situation always until you see a change.
The word of God is a powerful weapon to fight your battles.
Pray this morning with the word of God and speak it to all your situations; it is well with you.
Amen.
May the Lord bless you in Jesus name!

January 4

Good morning Father, Good morning Jesus, Good morning Holy Spirit.

Reading Passage
Ephesians 6:1-4

Find your watch Word
Ephesians 6:2,3 (Memorise)

Prayer
*God has commanded you to obey your parents, as well as your parents in the Lord.
That is, your pastors, teachers and people of God.
Obedience is better than sacrifice.
Pray that the Lord will give you the grace for obedience today in all things. Amen.
May the Lord bless you in Jesus name!*

January 5

Good morning Father, Good morning Jesus, Good morning Holy Spirit.

Reading Passage
James 4:4-7

Find your watch Word
Psalms 66:20 (Memorise)

Prayer
Pray that the Lord will give you the grace to humble yourself every time.
He will teach you the way to listen to Him, and to heed His words. Amen.
May the Lord bless you in Jesus name!

January 6

Good morning Father, Good morning Jesus, Good morning Holy Spirit.

Reading Passage
Proverbs 4:1-6

Find your watch Word
Psalms 119:130 (Memorise)

Prayer
Pray that the Lord will set you up today in the power of His word.
The Lord show Himself strong in your situations today and forever. Amen.
May the Lord bless you in Jesus name!

January 7

Good morning Father, Good morning Jesus, Good morning Holy Spirit.

Reading Passage
Proverbs 24:27-29

Find your watch Word
Psalms 17:21 (Memorise)

Prayer
God is your increase and comforter.
Pray this morning that He will bring increase to you today in all your hands shall touch.
Pray to Him to comfort you on every side with His hands.
In your business, studies and your work, today you are increased in Jesus Christ's name.
Do not repay evil for evil.
May the Lord bless you in Jesus name!

January 8

Good morning Father, Good morning Jesus, Good morning Holy Spirit.

Reading Passage
Psalms 89:23-26

Find your watch Word
Psalms 89:24 (Memorise)

Prayer
*Lord, today beat down my foes before my face, and plague them who hate me.
Let my horn be exalted by thy name.
Be my salvation today everywhere that I go.
Hallelujah!
May the Lord bless you in Jesus name!*

January 9

Good morning Father, Good morning Jesus, Good morning Holy Spirit.

Reading Passage
Philippians 2:14-16

Find your watch Word
Philippians 4:13 (Memorise)

Prayer
Do not murmur or dispute with anybody.
This is to protect you, so you can be blameless and harmless.
You are in the light; not in the darkness. Hold forth the word of faith, and stay in the word of God to build up your faith.
Pray today that the Lord will empower your faith to give birth to your victory. Amen.
May the Lord bless you in Jesus name!

January 10

Good morning Father, Good morning Jesus, Good morning Holy Spirit.

Reading Passage
1Timothy 4:12

Find your watch Word
2 Timothy 2:19 (Memorise)

Prayer
Do not let any man or woman deceive you in any way.
Always call upon God and listen.
Pray that God will give you the grace to listen and obey Him.
It's only God's guidance that doesn't fail. But give time to Him daily.
He will teach you. God help me this morning to be fulfilled in my service. Amen.
May the Lord bless you in Jesus name!

January 11

Good morning Father, Good morning Jesus, Good morning Holy Spirit.

Reading Passage
Titus 2:7-8

Find your watch Word
James 1:19 (Memorise)

Prayer
Pray that God will make your word to be seasoned with grace, each time you talk to people. Pray that as you talk, nobody will see corruption and condemnation in what you say.
Sincerity will be seen in you, and Satan will be ashamed, because you have nothing evil to say, and he has no bad report of you to hold on to.
Amen.
May the Lord bless you in Jesus name!

January 12

Good morning Father, Good morning Jesus, Good morning Holy Spirit.

Reading Passage
John 6:53-56

Find your watch Word
Hebrews 11:6 (Memorise)

Prayer
You have to pray that God will give you understanding and knowledge about the Communion.
Wisdom is the accurate application of Knowledge. Before you can use the Communion, your faith should be strong and, (faith walked by love) pray that the Lord help you to love others.
When you take the Communion this morning which is the flesh and the blood of Jesus Christ, I pray you are healed in Jesus Name. Amen.
May the Lord bless you in Jesus name!

January 13

Good morning Father, Good morning Jesus, Good morning Holy Spirit.

Reading Passage
John 17:15-20

Find your watch Word
John 14:13 (Memorise)

Prayer
Jesus Christ prayed that you may be sanctified through Him, (the truth).
I want you to pray today that the Lord will sanctify you.
He has already prayed for you this morning in the reading passage.
Whatever you asked this morning is sealed by Jesus.
May the Lord bless you in Jesus name!

January 14

Good morning Father, Good morning Jesus, Good morning Holy Spirit.

Reading Passage
Acts 19:2-6

Find your watch Word
John 4:24 (Memorise)

Prayer
The Holy Spirit is a Divine Personality whom we must honour, love, worship, fellowship with and listen to.
This morning take time to pray in the spirit.
The Holy Spirit is a comforter who is your helper and energiser to help you to pray in the Holy Spirit.
Just feel calm and let the Holy Spirit flow through you so you can begin to speak. Open your mouth and pray, and God will teach you how to pray aright.
Thank the Holy Spirit for helping you today.
Amen.
May the Lord bless you in Jesus name!

January 15

Good morning Father, Good morning Jesus, Good morning Holy Spirit.

Reading Passage
Job 14:7-9

Find your watch Word
Job 14:9 (Memorise)

Prayer
The Lord Jesus Christ is an example when He died; He came back to life (resurrected).
So is every dead in our life will rise again and sprout and resurrect.
Your prayer today is: God let everything seen and unseen that is dead in my life, arise and resurrect in the name of Jesus.
Jesus died and rose again.
May this be your experience today in Jesus Christ's name. Amen.
May the Lord bless you in Jesus name!

January 16

Good morning Father, Good morning Jesus, Good morning Holy Spirit.

Reading Passage
Hebrews 12: 2-3

Find your watch Word
Hebrews 12:24 (Memorise)

Prayer
Jesus perfected all that concerned us with the covenant He had with us with His blood.
It's the blood of Jesus that speaks better things than the blood of Abel.
He used the blood to perfect things that concerns us.
The blood of Jesus is perfect and powerful. Fix your eyes on Jesus and always remind Him of the sacrifice He did for us with His blood.
Declare the blood of Jesus this morning and at night with all that belongs to you, call the blood of Jesus. Amen.
May the Lord bless you in Jesus name!

January 17

Good morning Father, Good morning Jesus, Good morning Holy Spirit.

Reading Passage
Mark 11:23-24

Find your watch Word
Psalms 2:8 (Memorise)

Prayer
*Ask anything this morning and God will give it to you.
Why are you disturbed by that situation?
God says 'Ask of me ... the uttermost parts of the earth for your possession'. It's all yours. Amen.
May the Lord bless you in Jesus name!*

January 18

Good morning Father, Good morning Jesus, Good morning, Holy Spirit.

Reading Passage
1 Kings 18:30-35

Find your watch Word
Psalms 50:15 (Memorise)

Prayer
The religion you belong to is not a cult. God doesn't need any man assistance in all His ways. He is God who is able and sufficient. Pray today that God will give you more knowledge about Himself. May the Lord bless you in Jesus name!

January 19

Good morning Father, Good morning Jesus, Good morning Holy Spirit.

Reading Passage
Isaiah 43:1-3

Find your watch Word
Isaiah 50:8 (Memorise)

Prayer
*No condemnation for you in Jesus Christ.
Pray that all evil plans today will not stand or come to pass.
May the Lord scatter any one that gathers against you today. Amen.
May the Lord bless you in Jesus name!*

January 20

Good morning Father, Good morning Jesus, Good morning Holy Spirit.

Reading Passage
Daniel 14:17-19

Find your watch Word
Romans 4:20 (Memorise)

Prayer
Pray for the confidence of God and boldness today.
Nothing should be able to stress you out today. You will not be depressed in Jesus name. Claim every blessing today in boldness. Amen.
May the Lord bless you in Jesus name!

January 21

Good morning Father, Good morning Jesus, Good morning Holy Spirit.

Reading Passage
Galatians 5:22-25

Find your watch Word
Galatians 6:17 (Memorise)

Prayer
Pray that the fruit of the spirit will be powerfully evident in you.
God will give you victory over every spirit of evil and fruits of Satan. Amen.
May the Lord bless you in Jesus name!

January 22

Good morning Father, Good morning Jesus, Good morning Holy Spirit.

Reading Passage
Colossians 3:12-14

Find your watch Word
1 John 2:9 (Memorise)

Prayer
Pray that God will give you a new spirit today to love others.
You cannot continue to hate people; it has got no gain. Hatred is a spirit.
You are not of God if you have no love for your neighbour.
May the Lord bless you in Jesus name!

January 23

Good morning Father, Good morning Jesus, Good morning Holy Spirit.

Reading Passage
2 Corinthians 3:17

Find your watch Word
2 Corinthians 3:17 (Memorise)

Prayer
Pray and declare and set yourself at liberty, because the Spirit of God is with you where you are.
You are set at liberty from all bondages today and forever. Amen.
May the Lord bless you in Jesus name!

January 24

Good morning Father, Good morning Jesus, Good morning Holy Spirit.

Reading Passage
Psalms 91:1-10

Find your watch Word
Psalms 91:9,10 (Memorise)

Prayer
*Sing a song to the Lord this morning to worship Him and give thanks to Him.
Tell Him He is your refuge and your habitation.
May the Lord bless you in Jesus name!*

January 25

Good morning Father, Good morning Jesus, Good morning Holy Spirit.

Reading Passage
Isaiah 60:15

Find your watch Word
Psalms 61:7 (Memorise)

Prayer
Pray for double today, in every of your circumstances.
You can mention them. In my school work, I receive double, in my health, I receive double...
Amen.
May the Lord bless you in Jesus name!

January 26

Good morning Father, Good morning Jesus, Good morning Holy Spirit.

Reading Passage
Acts 2: 1-5

Find your watch Word
Acts 2: 21 (Memorise)

Prayer
Call upon the name of the Lord, you will be delivered; you will be saved from all diseases. The name of Jesus is above every other name and situation in any life.
He is able. Amen.
May the Lord bless you in Jesus name!

January 27

Good morning Father, Good morning Jesus, Good morning Holy Spirit.

Reading Passage
Acts 2: 36-40

Find your watch Word
Acts 4:32 (Memorise)

Prayer
Pray today for the oneness of the Church of God.
The Trinity is not divided.
Pray today for unity among the brethren and saints.
The early Churches were together in 'love' sharing and none of them lacked anything.
The Church is supposed to be a place of refuge for the captives, pray for love and unity. Amen.
May the Lord bless you in Jesus name!

January 28

Good morning Father, Good morning Jesus, Good morning Holy Spirit.

Reading Passage
Acts 3:1-8

Find your watch Word
Acts 3:6 (Memorise)

Prayer
Today, this name, Jesus that made the man in the above passage strong can make you strong in all your weaknesses – spiritual, physical or psychological.
Pray for the strength of God in all areas of your life. Amen.
May the Lord bless you in Jesus name!

January 29

Good morning Father, Good morning Jesus, Good morning Holy Spirit.

Reading Passage
Psalms 103:1-5

Find your watch Word
Psalms 103:5 (Memorise)

Prayer
Say good things to the Lord this morning for He has satisfied your mouth with good things. Your mouth is blessed so whatsoever you say is established every time.
Your health and days are renewed like eagles.
Amen.
May the Lord bless you in Jesus name!

January 30

Good morning Father, Good morning Jesus, Good morning Holy Spirit.

Reading Passage
Psalms 105:16-25

Find your watch Word
Psalms 105:24 (Memorise)

Prayer
*God's word to you is, 'You are stronger than your enemies'.
Start to pray and confess that "I am stronger than my enemies, now and forever".
The mouth of the Lord has said it. Amen.
May the Lord bless you in Jesus name!*

January 31

Good morning Father, Good morning Jesus, Good morning Holy Spirit.

Reading Passage
Proverbs 10: 17

Find your watch Word
Psalms 8:36 (Memorise)

Prayer
Pray actively today, that Satan will not have joy over you today. Jesus said He prayed for Peter that Satan will not overcome him.
Before you step out everyday pray that Satan shall not have influence over you.
Confess your sins, including the hidden sins. Sin is an enemy of the Spirit of God. Amen.
May the Lord Bless you in Jesus Name!

February 1

Good morning Father, Good morning Jesus, Good morning Holy Spirit.

Reading Passage
Proverbs 10: 1-7

Find your watch Word
Proverbs 10:7 (Memorise)

Prayer
You are a student; the word of God said 'your memory is blessed'.
Receive this word today and say to yourself 'my memory is blessed in all areas of my life'.
Pray that you will excel in all you lay your hands on. Amen.
May the Lord bless you in Jesus name!

February 2

Good morning Father, Good morning Jesus, Good morning Holy Spirit.

Reading Passage
Psalms 116:7

Find your watch Word
Psalms 71:8 (Memorise)

Prayer
Pray today that the Lord is with your soul; say it prophetically.
Cast your care unto the Lord for He cares for you.
Praise Him from the depth of your heart.
Rest completely on Him; tell the Lord that He should unfold His unfailing love to you for you hope in His mercy. Amen.
May the Lord bless you in Jesus name!

February 3

Good morning Father, Good morning Jesus, Good morning Holy Spirit.

Reading Passage
Psalms 84:11-12

Find your watch Word
Psalms 84:11 (Memorise)

Prayer
Lord Jesus, give unto me the grace of "uprightness" before thee.
Let my way be perfect in you. Create in me a new heart that will lead to your glory as I go out today. Amen.
May the Lord bless you in Jesus name!

February 4

Good morning Father, Good morning Jesus, Good morning Holy Spirit.

Reading Passage
Matthew 16:19

Find your watch Word
Psalms 31:1 (Memorise)

Prayer
Lord Jesus, I look up unto you today. Let me not be put to shame. Let my inner eyes be flooded with your light today. I refuse to be put to shame today in Jesus name. Amen.
May the Lord bless you in Jesus name!

February 5

Good morning Father, Good morning Jesus, Good morning Holy Spirit.

Reading Passage
Psalms 23

Find your watch Word
Job 28:28 (Memorise)

Prayer
The Lord that declares the end from the beginning let my inner eyes be flooded with understanding of your glory. Amen.
May the Lord bless you in Jesus name!

February 6

Good morning Father, Good morning Jesus, Good morning Holy Spirit.

Reading Passage
Acts 15: 8-11

Find your watch Word
Acts 13:37 (Memorise)

Prayer
Jesus Christ the Son of the living God, this morning I declare I will see no corruption. You who know the heart acknowledge me by your Holy Spirit today. Amen.
May the Lord bless you in Jesus name!

February 7

Good morning Father, Good morning Jesus, Good morning Holy Spirit.

Reading Passage
Lamentations 3:31-33

Find your watch Word
Lamentations 3:40 (Memorise)

Prayer
*Father, examine me today and my ways; search me and deliver me from problems.
You are good to those who wait for you.
Have mercy on me this morning. Amen.
May the Lord bless you in Jesus name!*

February 8

Good morning Father, Good morning Jesus, Good morning Holy Spirit.

Reading Passage
Acts 19:8-13

Find your watch Word
Acts 19:11 (Memorise)

Prayer
Today God will work unusual miracles in your life.
The miracles you do not expect God will put them in your endeavours.
Pray as you go out today, and call all unusual miracles your way. Amen.
May the Lord bless you in Jesus name!

February 9

Good morning Father, Good morning Jesus, Good morning Holy Spirit.

Reading Passage
Acts 18:7-10

Find your watch Word
Acts 18:9b-10a (Memorise)

Prayer
*Do not be afraid. Pray and rebuke every spirit of fear that Satan might want to use today to hold you captive in any area of your life.
Carry the presence of God and preach the Gospel to the world. Do not keep silent. Amen.
May the Lord bless you in Jesus name!*

February 10

Good morning Father, Good morning Jesus, Good morning Holy Spirit.

Reading Passage
Acts 20: 1,29-35

Find your watch Word
Acts 20:35 (Memorise)

Prayer
*Pray that the Lord will grant you understanding to give to people than to receive.
Give to the poor. Amen.
May the Lord bless you in Jesus name!*

February 11

Good morning Father, Good morning Jesus, Good morning Holy Spirit.

Reading Passage
Isaiah 48: 15-17

Find your watch Word
Isaiah 48:17 (Memorise)

Prayer
*The Lord has thought me to prosper.
I will prosper. Today is my prosperity day.
I will not fail. I am destined to prosper.
May the Lord bless you in Jesus name!*

February 12

Good morning Father, Good morning Jesus, Good morning Holy Spirit.

Reading Passage
Jeremiah 5:24-31

Find your watch Word
Jeremiah 5:29 (Memorise)

Prayer
Pray today that God will avenge you from all your adversaries.
He will not leave them alone but fight on your behalf and deliver you from their hands. Amen.
May the Lord bless you in Jesus name!

February 13

Good morning Father, Good morning Jesus, Good morning Holy Spirit.

Reading Passage
Jeremiah 17:7-10

Find your watch Word
Jeremiah 17:8 (Memorise)

Prayer
Decree this morning that you are a tree planted by the waters and that spread out her roots by the river, and shall not see when heat comes, but that your leaves shall be green and not be anxious in the year of drought. Amen.
May the Lord bless you in Jesus name!

February 14

Good morning Father, Good morning Jesus, Good morning Holy Spirit.

Reading Passage
2 Thessalonians 3:2-6

Find your watch Word
2 Thessalonians 3:3 (Memorise)

Prayer
The Lord is able to keep you safe from evil in the night and day.
He will establish you.
Pray that the faithful God will establish and keep you. Amen.
May the Lord bless you in Jesus name!

February 15

Good morning Father, Good morning Jesus, Good morning Holy Spirit.

Reading Passage
1 Peter 5:6-10

Find your watch Word
1 Peter 5:7 (Memorise)

Prayer
Pray today with all your might that God will always give you the enablement to "cast your care on Jesus".
Satan your adversary is watching your carelessness to put burden on you. Amen.
May the Lord bless you in Jesus name!

February 16

Good morning Father, Good morning Jesus, Good morning Holy Spirit.

Reading Passage
2 Peter 1:1-7

Find your watch Word
2 Peter 1:3 (Memorise)

Prayer
I call upon the Lord concerning my circumstances, everything that is pertaining to life and godliness I receive now, in the name of the Father, the Son and the Holy Spirit.
Let your glory shine upon my life in Jesus name.
Amen.
May the Lord bless you in Jesus name!

February 17

Good morning Father, Good morning Jesus, Good morning Holy Spirit.

Reading Passage
Revelation 1: 16-18

Find your watch Word
Revelation 1:18 (Memorise)

Prayer
The Lord is the first and the last; He is the master planner of your life.
Call upon Him today, to order everything that concerns you unto the honour of His name.
He is able to do all things.
May the Lord Bless you in Jesus Name!

February 18

Good morning Father, Good morning Jesus, Good morning Holy Spirit.

Reading Passage
Ezekiel 17: 9-12

Find your watch Word
Ezekiel 17:12 (Memorise)

Prayer
Pray according to the Find your watch Word today.
That the Lord will cause life to flow into every area of your life that rebellion and disobedience has caused to die in the name of Jesus.
That the Lord will grant you the grace to work in obedience, so that you will remain consistent, and Satan will not have dominion over you any longer.
May the Lord bless you in Jesus name!

February 19

Good morning Father, Good morning Jesus, Good morning Holy Spirit.

Reading Passage
Hebrews 10: 34-36

Find your watch Word
Hebrews 10:35 (Memorise)

Prayer
Do not be weak in courage; wait for the Lord and His plans for your life.
Remember the scripture says: 'Do not throw away your confidence in the Lord'.
Wake up unto your confidence and ask the Lord to give you a new spirit and a new heart.
Do not keep quiet, ask the Lord for your need today. He is always waiting to hear from you, ask Him for your need today and God bless you as you do. Amen.
May the Lord bless you in Jesus name!

February 20

Good morning Father, Good morning Jesus, Good morning Holy Spirit.

Reading Passage
Ephesians 4: 29-32

Find your watch Word
Ephesians 5: 11 (Memorise)

Prayer
*Today the Lord needs you to quit all fellowship you have with works of the darkness.
It is shameful to even speak of them in your life. God wants you to carry His light and not darkness. Let no corrupt words proceed out of your mouth, malice, bitterness, wrath and lots of evil works. Declare yourself free from them today. May the Lord bless you in Jesus name!*

February 21

Good morning Father, Good morning Jesus, Good morning Holy Spirit.

Reading Passage
Hebrews 2: 1-3

Find your watch Word
Hebrews 2:2 (Memorise)

Prayer
Rebuke the spirit of disobedience this morning and pray that God should open your eyes and enlighten your understanding that you will surrender yourself to His will.
Pray for supernatural grace from God.
You are blessed. Amen.
May the Lord bless you in Jesus name!

February 22

Good morning Father, Good morning Jesus, Good morning Holy Spirit.

Reading Passage
Isaiah 54:17

Find your watch Word
Isaiah 54:17 (Memorise)

Prayer
Your prayer today is that you will be established in righteousness and that you will be far removed from oppression of the enemy.
Your speaking word today is that no weapon formed against you shall prosper. Amen.
May the Lord bless you in Jesus name!

February 23

Good morning Father, Good morning Jesus, Good morning Holy Spirit.

Reading Passage
Jeremiah 32:21-27

Find your watch Word
Jeremiah 32:27 (Memorise)

Prayer
Pray today that the Lord of all flesh of which nothing is too hard would make every hard thing in your life answer to His honour and possibility. Pray that every difficult door be opened to you today and forever.
May the Lord bless you in Jesus name!

February 24

Good morning Father, Good morning Jesus, Good morning Holy Spirit.

Reading Passage
Obadiah 1:13-17

Find your watch Word
Obadiah 1:17 (Memorise)

Prayer
Stand against every gate standing against your possession. The scripture said: 'Upon Mount Zion there shall be deliverance and holiness and you will posses your possessions'. Today is the day of your possession'.
What are they?
Mention them and call them forth, success, job, good health, your destiny cannot be relegated, because you are a child of promise.
Amen.
May the Lord bless you in Jesus name!

February 25

Good morning Father, Good morning Jesus, Good morning Holy Spirit.

Reading Passage
Joel 2:25-27

Find your watch Word
Joel 2:25 (Memorise)

Prayer
Pray that the Lord will restore to you the years that the swarming locust has eaten in your life. Call all your success, money, health. That Satan has eaten up, back to you. Amen. May the Lord bless you in Jesus name!

February 26

Good morning Father, Good morning Jesus, Good morning Holy Spirit.

Reading Passage
Malachi 4:1-3

Find your watch Word
Malachi 4:2 (Memorise)

Prayer
Do you fear the Lord; the Son of righteousness will arise with healing in His wings and surprise you.
Ask the Lord to heal you in all areas of your life.
Amen.
May the Lord bless you in Jesus name!

February 27

Good morning Father, Good morning Jesus, Good morning Holy Spirit.

Reading Passage
Psalms 86:16-17

Find your watch Word
Psalms 86:17 (Memorise)

Prayer
Ask the Lord to show you a sign this time around. Pray for a sign of victory, a sign of Joy and a sign of miracles. Amen.
May the Lord Bless you in Jesus Name!

February 28

Good morning Father, Good morning Jesus, Good morning Holy Spirit.

Reading Passage
Psalms 92:10-15

Find your watch Word
Psalms 92:10 (Memorise)

Prayer
Pray that the Lord will lift up your horn like a wild ox today. What are you expecting the Lord to do for you?
The Bible says: 'All things are possible for him who believes for with God nothing shall be impossible'. Amen.
May the Lord Bless you in Jesus Name!

February 29

Good morning Father, Good morning Jesus, Good morning Holy Spirit.

Reading Passage
Psalm25 : 12-15

Find your watch Word
Ps.25: 14-15 (Memorise)

Prayer
The fear of the Lord is the beginning of all things. Without the fear of God in our lives then life is just a waste.
The book of Josuah 1 : 8 says meditate in the word day and night.
May the Lord bless you in Jesus name!

March 1

Good morning Father, Good morning Jesus, Good morning Holy Spirit.

Reading Passage
Proverbs 9: 7-11

Find your watch Word
Proverbs 9:9 (Memorise)

Prayer
*Lord Jesus I humble myself at Your instruction today. Instruct me in Your righteousness. I will not go against Your directions.
Have mercy on me that I might rejoice in You.
Amen.
May the Lord bless you in Jesus name!*

March 2

Good morning Father, Good morning Jesus, Good morning Holy Spirit.

Reading Passage
Proverbs 10: 19-21

Find your watch Word
Proverbs 10:19-21 (Memorise)

Prayer
Is your word a choice silver? Answer Yes or No to this question.
Pray that the Lord will give you grace, knowledge and wisdom to make your word few.
Always let that word be few, that you might be able to say what God is saying. Amen.
May the Lord bless you in Jesus name!

March 3

Good morning Father, Good morning Jesus, Good morning Holy Spirit.

Reading Passage
Lamentations 3: 31-33

Find your watch Word
LAmentations 3:32 (Memorise)

Prayer
Father in the mighty name of Jesus show me compassion in the multitude of your mercies. You will not break your covenant but you will remember it in Your mercy. Amen
May the Lord bless you in Jesus name!

March 4

Good morning Father, Good morning Jesus, Good morning Holy Spirit.

Reading Passage
John 17: 9-17

Find your watch Word
John 17:17 (Memorise)

Prayer
The word of God is truth. Learn as much as possible each day; hold tightly to the word of God. The Lord will be glorified in you through the Word He has given us.

When you want to read the word of God, pray for God to give the word to pray and confess. Amen. May the Lord bless you in Jesus name!

March 5

Good morning Father, Good morning Jesus, Good morning Holy Spirit.

Reading Passage
John 18:7-11

Find your watch Word
John 18:8 (Memorise)

Prayer
Always learn to seek the Lord Jesus. Every other thing will fall in place for you, when you seek Him.
Peter was very active among the twelve closest to the Lord Jesus.
Pray that God will give you the grace to seek the Lord Jesus always.
In the scripture if anything was going to happen to Peter, Jesus Christ would see it and pray for him, because of the closeness. Amen.
May the Lord bless you in Jesus name!

March 6

Good morning Father, Good morning Jesus, Good morning Holy Spirit.

Reading Passage
Acts 4:13-17

Find your watch Word
Acts 4:16 (Memorise)

Prayer
The Lord wrought a notable miracle in the midst of His people.
Ask the Lord for your own notable miracle in this month of March.
It should not come to an end except your own notable miracle comes around. Amen.
May the Lord bless you in Jesus name!

March 7

Good morning Father, Good morning Jesus, Good morning Holy Spirit.

Reading Passage
Hebrews 10:16-24

Find your watch Word
Hebrews 10:16 (Memorise)

Prayer
The Lord has promised to give you a new heart and a new spirit.
Are you guilty of some sins that you have committed?
Do not forget the Lord has promised to give you a new heart and your sins of lawless deeds He will not remember again.
Receive the new heart and new spirit in Jesus name. Amen.
May the Lord bless you in Jesus name!

March 8

Good morning Father, Good morning Jesus, Good morning Holy Spirit.

Reading Passage
Proverbs 12: 17-20

Find your watch Word
Proverbs 12:17 (Memorise)

Prayer
*Are you after righteousness? You need to pray for grace to always speak the truth.
Jesus Christ is our truth. Anybody that is deceitful does not know the Lord.
Keep truth so that you might be exalted in righteousness. Amen.
May the Lord bless you in Jesus name!*

March 9

Good morning Father, Good morning Jesus, Good morning Holy Spirit.

Reading Passage
Proverbs 26: 13-16

Find your watch Word
Proverbs 26:16 (Memorise)

Prayer
Rebuke the spirit of laziness and work out your confidence through God in all areas.
Tell yourself 'I can do it'.
Satan can deceive you, giving you different types of stories and putting fear in your heart to cast you down.
The Lord said to the children of Israel 'Go Forward'.
Pray laziness out of your way today. Amen.
May the Lord bless you in Jesus name!

March 10

Good morning Father, Good morning Jesus, Good morning Holy Spirit.

Reading Passage
1 Corinthians 13:1-7

Find your watch Word
1 Corinthians 13: 4-7 (Memorise)

Prayer
Pray for the grace for love, to love the Lord with all your heart, might and to love those people around you.
Christ is the end of the law; and whoever loves another has fulfilled the law.
Without love, remember you are living in death.
Satan is looking for those who don't understand the mystery of love.
Ask the Lord to give you the understanding and knowledge of love.
Give thanks to God for the answered prayer.
Amen.
May the Lord bless you in Jesus name!

March 11

Good morning Father, Good morning Jesus, Good morning Holy Spirit.

Reading Passage
Colossians 3: 10-12

Find your watch Word
Colossians 3:12 (Memorise)

Prayer
Jesus Christ our example of honesty had humility and meekness.
You must be meek as Jesus is, so that when you call upon Jesus it will work for you.
The name 'Jesus' is a strong tower, without meekness your prayer may not be answered.
Pray for the grace today that God will teach you.
Amen.
May the Lord bless you in Jesus name!

March 12

Good morning Father, Good morning Jesus, Good morning Holy Spirit.

Reading Passage
Zephaniah 2:1-3

Find your watch Word
Zephaniah 2:3 (Memorise)

Prayer
Pray for God's righteous spirit to come into you this morning.
You must be righteous as your Father in heaven is righteous.
Remember without holiness and righteousness no one shall see the Lord. Amen.
May the Lord bless you in Jesus name!

March 13

Good morning Father, Good morning Jesus, Good morning Holy Spirit.

Reading Passage
Acts 15:16; Proverbs 19:21

Find your watch Word
Proverbs 19:21 (Memorise)

Prayer
Remember the scripture says that it is the counsel of the Lord that shall stand.
Let the counsel of the Lord stand in your life.
This cannot be done except you call upon the name of Jesus in truth.
He has the map for your life and plan.
Pray this morning that you surrender yourself to Him and that His counsel concerning you should stand.
Give thanks to the Lord for He has taken the counsel of your life and you will never regret it.
Amen.
May the Lord bless you in Jesus name!

March 14

Good morning Father, Good morning Jesus, Good morning Holy Spirit.

Reading Passage
Ephesians 4:32; Colossians 3:13

Find your watch Word
Ephesians 4:32 (Memorise)

Prayer
Remember the scripture is emphasising the issue of forgiveness.
You need to think seriously and think before you pray this morning, so that your own sins will be forgiven.
Pray that God will help you because without forgiveness of sins your prayer cannot be heard by God.
Clear the ground that your prayer can go quickly up to the throne of grace. Amen.
May the Lord bless you in Jesus name!

March 15

Good morning Father, Good morning Jesus, Good morning Holy Spirit.

Reading Passage
Galatians 5:21-23

Find your watch Word
Galatians 5: 21-23 (Memorise)

Prayer
The work of kindness has a spiritual dimension as a fruit of the spirit.
Naturally, it's difficult to be kind, more so when there is nothing to benefit from it.
Our model for kindness is Jesus the Son of God.
Kindness is one of the marks of a child of God.
What are you going to do about this today?
Your strength in Jesus is the ability to be kind.
Ask the Lord to deposit the seed of kindness in you today so that you can prosper in your work of the spirit. Amen.
May the Lord bless you in Jesus name!

March 16

Good morning Father, Good morning Jesus, Good morning Holy Spirit.

Reading Passage
Philippians 2: 8-11

Find your watch Word
Philippians 2: 10 (Memorise)

Prayer
At the name of Jesus every knee must bow. The name of Jesus is an authority in Heaven and on Earth.
Call the name of 'Jesus' with all seriousness, this morning over everything that is hindering you in your daily undertaking and your future.
When you call 'Jesus' let it have a root on your spirit and add your strong and stubborn 'Faith'.
He will answer you by fire.
Try it today and you will return to Him with thanksgiving. Amen.
May the Lord bless you in Jesus name!

March 17

Good morning Father, Good morning Jesus, Good morning Holy Spirit.

Reading Passage
Acts 19:11-13

Find your watch Word
Acts 19: 11 (Memorise)

Prayer
God must work unusual miracles in your life this week, this month and even this year.
Call upon Him this morning and ask Him for 'miracles' that are unusual.
Tell Him Father I want an unusual miracle. Pray for it and believe.
He never fails. He will make you a wonder.
He is always giving it out to those who love Him.
Amen.
May the Lord bless you in Jesus name!

March 18

Good morning Father, Good morning Jesus, Good morning Holy Spirit.

Reading Passage
Isaiah 9:6-8

Find your watch Word
Isaiah 9:6 (Memorise)

Prayer
The Lord Jesus is the Prince of Peace.
Are you troubled in your heart?
Ask Him for your peace this morning, He gives
His peace freely not as the world gives.
Receive it into your life today.
Let all the troubled waters in your life cease now.
You are the help of my life. Amen.
May the Lord bless you in Jesus name!

March 19

Good morning Father, Good morning Jesus, Good morning Holy Spirit.

Reading Passage
Acts 19:11-17

Find your watch Word
Acts 19:17 (Memorise)

Prayer
Pray that God will give you a testimony today. Those that believe came, to testify to the power of God.
Your enemies will be put under your feet and you will testify in Jesus Name. Amen.
May the Lord bless you in Jesus name!

March 20

Good morning Father, Good morning Jesus, Good morning Holy Spirit.

Reading Passage
Romans 8:31-37

Find your watch Word
Romans 8:35 (Memorise)

Prayer
Who can separate you from the love of Christ Jesus?
The scripture says you are more than conqueror through Him (Christ) that loves you. Pray to the Lord that nothing should be able to separate you from the love of Christ Jesus.
He is able to deliver you; call Him this morning that all hindrances be removed from your way as you journey to your Canaan Land.
Receive it in Jesus name. Amen.
May the Lord bless you in Jesus name!

March 21

Good morning Father, Good morning Jesus, Good morning Holy Spirit.

Reading Passage
Hebrews 12:1-3

Find your watch Word
Hebrews 12:2 (Memorise)

Prayer
Look unto Jesus; don't look unto man because man will fail you.
The scripture says: 'Woe unto him that put his trust in man'.
Don't serve man but serve God.
He is the God that is able to make way for you.
Pray that God creates in you a new heart of wanting to return to Jesus always before taking any step in life. Amen.
May the Lord bless you in Jesus name!

March 22

Good morning Father, Good morning Jesus, Good morning Holy Spirit.

Reading Passage
John 1:1-5

Find your watch Word
John 1:3 (Memorise)

Prayer
There is nothing you can do without Jesus. The Bible says without Him nothing was made. So pray today that God who had made you, will make your life's destiny work out for you. Today He will make your helper to walk your way.
Hallelujah! Amen.
May the Lord bless you in Jesus name!

March 23

Good morning Father, Good morning Jesus, Good morning Holy Spirit.

Reading Passage
Psalms 9: 9-10

Find your watch Word
Psalms 9:10 (Memorise)

Prayer
The promises of God are ye and Amen.
The Bible said those who seek you, you will not forsake.
Tell the Lord and return His word back to Him.
Lord you have not forsaken those who seek you.
Remember me Oh Lord today in my captivity.
Amen.
May the Lord bless you in Jesus name!

March 24

Good morning Father, Good morning Jesus, Good morning Holy Spirit.

Reading Passage
Psalms 95:2-8

Find your watch Word
Psalms 95:8 (Memorise)

Prayer
Father God, speak to me today; let me hear your voice.
I refuse to harden my heart.
I receive the grace of obedience to your directions.
Give me a hearing ear that obey and the eyes that focus. Speak to the Lord in your prayers.
He is near you. Amen.
May the Lord bless you in Jesus name!

March 25

Good morning Father, Good morning Jesus, Good morning Holy Spirit.

Reading Passage
1 Corinthians 1:26-31

Find your watch Word
1 Corinthians 1:29-31 (Memorise)

Prayer
Children of God, Jesus is the wisdom, righteousness, sanctification and the redemption of God for us.
We can only glory in Christ.
Sinless, self-abased, murmuring free flesh is proud and take self glory even in the presence of God.
Faith cut off all pride and self glory.
Glory only in Christ. Amen.
May the Lord bless you in Jesus name!

March 26

Good morning Father, Good morning Jesus, Good morning Holy Spirit.

Reading Passage
1 Timothy 6:11

Find your watch Word
1 Timothy 6:11 (Memorise)

Prayer
The word of the Lord is a delight unto us.
Pray today that God will provide you with the knowledge you need to prevail spiritually and physically.
Remember the word of God is a light unto the feet of the saint.
Let the word of God dwell in you richly. Pray for favour and the grace of God to abide by His words. Amen.
May the Lord bless you in Jesus name!

March 27

Good morning Father, Good morning Jesus, Good morning Holy Spirit.

Reading Passage
1 Timothy 4:11-14

Find your watch Word
1 Timothy 4:12 (Memorise)

Prayer
The word of the Lord said let no man despise your youth.
Keep away from everyone that put the corruptible input in the life of the children of God.
You have the will to stop yourself from bad inputs. Don't stop reading.
The word of God said you should give attention to reading, exhorting and doctrine.
Pray that the Lord will give you the grace of stability in the spirit, knowledge, understanding and wisdom and the counsel of God.
Read scriptural books, study your bible. Amen.
May the Lord bless you in Jesus name!

March 28

Good morning Father, Good morning Jesus, Good morning Holy Spirit.

Reading Passage
Hebrews 10:24-26

Find your watch Word
Hebrews 10:24 (Memorise)

Prayer
Pray for the grace to love. The word of God is tells us not to forsake the assembly of ourselves; and promote good work and love.
Love is very important in the house of the Lord. It encapsulates the laws of God.
Satan strives to take us away from the assembly of the children of God.
What Satan does is try to isolate us to be able to punish us.
The Lord will give you the wisdom above the enemy.
Keep attending the fellowship and love the children of God.
Pray to the Lord on these issues.Amen.
May the Lord bless you in Jesus name!

March 29

Good morning Father, Good morning Jesus, Good morning Holy Spirit.

Reading Passage
1 Corinthians 2:12-15

Find your watch Word
1 Corinthians 2:13 (Memorise)

Prayer
The Bible says that a lot has been given to us freely by God.
It's the Holy Spirit that can enlighten us in those things.
God gives everything freely to us.
We can only perceive these things by our spiritual eyes and not with the natural eyes.
The natural eyes see only the physical.
So he who sees in the natural goes through stresses, troubles and can never be delivered except by the Spirit of God who guides and directs.
May the Lord strengthen our spiritual eyes, confidence and faith to possess our possession.
Pray it out loud today and go for it. Amen.
May the Lord bless you in Jesus name!

March 30

Good morning Father, Good morning Jesus, Good morning Holy Spirit.

Reading Passage
Song of Solomon 8:6

Find your watch Word
Song of Solomon 8:6 (Memorise)

Prayer
Pray that the love of God be multiplied to you. Run away from jealousy because it's a destroyer. Always seek to love God and His kingdom and in it you will be able to multiply in love. Amen
May the Lord bless you in Jesus name!

March 31

Good morning Father, Good morning Jesus, Good morning Holy Spirit.

Reading Passage
Song of Solomon 2:2-4

Find your watch Word
Song of Solomon 2:4 (Memorise)

Prayer
*Think on the Find your watch Word from today.
Let the Lord minister to you.
Then pray according to how the Spirit leads you.
Jesus brings you to the banqueting table.
This is where everything is ready for you to just sit down and eat. Hallelujah! Amen.
May the Lord bless you in Jesus name!*

April 1

Good morning Father, Good morning Jesus, Good morning Holy Spirit.

Reading passage
Leviticus 19:16-19

Find your watch Word
Leviticus 19:16 (Memorise)

Prayer
They said you shall not be a tale bearer among your people.
What is your role in the house of God?
Are you a tale bearer at work and wherever you find yourself?
God will help you. It can block your entrance unto the throne of grace.
Only be the keeper of God's commands - turn it to prayer today. Amen.
May the Lord bless you in Jesus name!

April 2

Good morning Father, Good morning Jesus, Good morning Holy Spirit.

Reading passage
Proverbs 10:11-13

Find your watch Word
Proverbs 10:11a (Memorise)

Prayer
The Bible commands us to love and to live righteous, a person who lives a balanced life. He loves his neighbour not in sin, strife or hatred. Pray that the Lord will help you to live a life that is worthy of His praise and grace.
There is nothing impossible for God to do.
Your life does not belong to you.
It is of God. You are what you are by the grace of God.
Pray according to the direction of the Holy Spirit.
Amen.
May the Lord bless you in Jesus name!

April 3

Good morning Father, Good morning Jesus, Good morning Holy Spirit.

Reading passage
Matthew 5:33-37

Find your watch Word
Matthew 5:34 (Memorise)

Prayer
The Bible commands us not to swear; it says let your yes be "yes" and your no be "no".
To me the interpretation of this is "do not lie".
Anyone whose word is not stable is a liar.
A liar will not enter the kingdom of God.
Train your tongue to tell the truth.
May the Lord help you take the decision today for a drastic change in your lifestyle. Amen.
May the Lord bless you in Jesus name!

April 4

Good morning Father, Good morning Jesus, Good morning Holy Spirit.

Reading passage
John 5:28-30

Find your watch Word
John 5:30a (Memorise)

Prayer
*You cannot do anything outside of God.
The confession of apostle Paul was 'I can do all things through Christ who strengthens me'.
Call upon me the Lord says and I will answer you.
Pray that the Lord will help you do away with struggle.
Give all your struggles to God, for you cannot do anything without Him.
God will help you, you will not regret it. Amen.
May the Lord bless you in Jesus name!*

April 5

Good morning Father, Good morning Jesus, Good morning Holy Spirit.

Reading passage
2 Corinthians 6:14-18

Find your watch Word
2 Corinthians 6:14c (Memorise)

Prayer
You cannot be for God and have association with the darkness.
Light and darkness are not related.
The temple of God does not relate to idols.
You should cut off from every evil communion.
God will not dwell in you or walk among you unless you come out of the multitude as you continue to walk in the Lord and light.
You will see the Lord's hand all around you. God bless you. Amen.
May the Lord bless you in Jesus name!

April 6

Good morning Father, Good morning Jesus, Good morning Holy Spirit.

Reading passage
2 Corinthians 4:16-18

Find your watch Word
2 Corinthians 4:18c (Memorise)

Prayer
For the things which are seen are temporal and the ones unseen are eternal.
We should always set our eyes and mind on the things which are not seen.
This world is for a short time.
As long as we live let us put our trust in the Lord for all things that we desire.
He is our reward.
Pray for the renewal of your mind and spirit today and stand firm in the Lord. Amen.
May the Lord bless you in Jesus name!

April 7

Good morning Father, Good morning Jesus, Good morning Holy Spirit.

Reading passage
Proverbs 16:3-5

Find your watch Word
Proverbs 16:3 (Memorise)

Prayer
The Lord wants you to commit your ways unto Him today so that He can establish your thoughts in all ways.
Call upon Him so as to receive the grace for today.
By yourself you can do nothing. Amen.
May the Lord bless you in Jesus name!

April 8

Good morning Father, Good morning Jesus, Good morning Holy Spirit.

Reading passage
Proverbs 16:20-22

Find your watch Word
Proverbs 16:22 (Memorise)

Prayer
Refuse to be a fool today, get yourself understanding.
Read the word of God fervently and receive the Spirit of understanding to do what He has commanded you to do.
The Lord said if you love me, you will keep my commandments.
Receive the anointing to keep God's commandment today so you can walk in your high places. Amen.
May the Lord bless you in Jesus name!

April 9

Good morning Father, Good morning Jesus, Good morning Holy Spirit.

Reading passage
Isaiah 26:5, 8-9

Find your watch Word
Isaiah 26:3 (Memorise)

Prayer
The Lord has sent His word and the word of God will accomplish His will.
He will keep you in perfect peace, those whose minds stay on Him.
Glorify the Lord in your mortal body.
Let your heart and mind stay on Him.
I prophesy this morning your peace is guaranteed.
Pray and receive it.
May the Lord bless you. Amen.
May the Lord bless you in Jesus name!

April 10

Good morning Father, Good morning Jesus, Good morning Holy Spirit.

Reading passage
2 Timothy 3:14-16

Find your watch Word
2 Timothy 3:16 (Memorise)

Prayer
*The Word of God should be your focus.
Teach yourself diligently in this.
Let the word of God wash you, cleanse you and lighten your way all day.
Prove yourself in it, it will always lead you.
Without God you cannot do anything.
Pray for grace to align with the word of God as you study today. Amen.
May the Lord bless you in Jesus name!*

April 11

Good morning Father, Good morning Jesus, Good morning Holy Spirit.

Reading passage
2 Timothy 3:4-16

Find your watch Word
2 Timothy 3: 14 (Memorise)

Prayer
You should always ask yourself if you are putting the Word of God into use.
The Bible is calling your attention to those things you have learnt.
Are you putting the Word of God to action; that is, doing them or you are doing the contrary?
Know where you have learnt them.
Do not let anybody turn the pure Word of God to joke or play.
Let the word of God you have learnt be your first priority.
Eat the Word, digest them and chant them daily and live on them.
Cry to God this morning for the grace of God that never ceases. Amen.
May the Lord bless you in Jesus name!

April 12

Good morning Father, Good morning Jesus, Good morning Holy Spirit.

Reading passage
Proverbs 10: 22-28

Find your watch Word
Proverbs 10:27-28 (Memorise)

Prayer
The fear of the Lord prolongs years.
Without the fear of God, life will be shortened because man will be living without guide and light.
The scripture says that apart from long life, the hope of a righteous man is gladness.
Only God can give a meaningful gladness.
May you live long and have meaningful gladness.
The Lord of Host will grant you the grace unto the entry into abundance. Amen.
May the Lord bless you in Jesus name!

April 13

Good morning Father, Good morning Jesus, Good morning Holy Spirit.

Reading passage
Proverbs 4:16-18

Find your watch Word
Proverbs 4: 18 (Memorise)

Prayer
The path of the righteous man is like a shinning sun.
The scripture says it shines and ever brighter unto the perfect day.
The righteous man is upright in all his ways. Who are you?
Can you boast of your own way?
Is it shining or is it dark?
Remember the Bible says that the way of the wicked is darkness.
The Lord will give you understanding to His word.
The Holy Spirit will teach you how to pray today. Amen.
May the Lord bless you in Jesus name!

April 14

Good morning Father, Good morning Jesus, Good morning Holy Spirit.

Reading passage
Psalms 67:5-7

Find your watch Word
Psalms 67:6 (Memorise)

Prayer
Call upon the name of God, praise Him again and again and the Earth will yield her increase. Say to yourself that the Earth shall yield her increase to me today.
There must be testimony of God's increase in a particular area of your life. Amen.
May the Lord bless you in Jesus name!

April 15

Good morning Father, Good morning Jesus, Good morning Holy Spirit.

Reading passage
Psalms 68:9-11

Find your watch Word
Psalms 68:11 (Memorise)

Prayer
Great was the company of those who proclaim the Word of God.
Are you one of those who are ready to proclaim the Word of God?
Preach the Gospel to others and you will not lose your reward.
Do not keep silent that you and your children shall be great.
Tell God to increase your greatness and preach the gospel to others today (Psalms 71:21). Amen.
May the Lord bless you in Jesus name!

April 16

Good morning Father, Good morning Jesus, Good morning Holy Spirit.

Reading passage
Deuteronomy 32:10-12

Find your watch Word
Deuteronomy 32:10b (Memorise)

Prayer
This is the day the Lord has made. Pray that the Lord should encompass you, instruct you and keep you as the apple of His eye.
Do not go about without the instruction of God. He will enable you with His Spirit and you will prosper. Amen.
May the Lord bless you in Jesus name!

April 17

Good morning Father, Good morning Jesus, Good morning Holy Spirit.

Reading passage
Job 13:14-16

Find your watch Word
Job 13:16 (Memorise)

Prayer
The Lord will be your salvation but remember that hypocrites could not come before Him. For God to be your salvation, you need to take your stand in Him.
Make God proud of you.
God your keeper will surround you by Himself.
Amen.
May the Lord bless you in Jesus name!

April 18

Good morning Father, Good morning Jesus, Good morning Holy Spirit.

Reading passage
2 Corinthians 2:11-17

Find your watch Word
2 Corinthians 2:14 (Memorise)

Prayer
God makes us to triumph through Christ in all we do through the knowledge of Christ but not by ourselves.
Jesus Christ has made a complete sacrifice for us. Today you have full knowledge in Him to do all things. Glory be to God (Hallelujah).
Nothing can be impossible, hold firmly the word of triumph through Christ and put any impossible area of your life to God and keep confessing it that I triumph through the knowledge of Christ in my finance, academic, etc, Amen.
May the Lord bless you in Jesus name!

April 19

Good morning Father, Good morning Jesus, Good morning Holy Spirit.

Reading passage
Psalms 103:19-22

Find your watch Word
Psalms 103:22a (Memorise)

Prayer
Praise the Lord at all times.
God is worthy to be praised in all places.
God's dominion is in all places so He is not limited in praise.
Everywhere is the place of dominion of the Lord.
Open your heart and your mouth and sing praises to the Lord of peace.
This is the place of dominion where you are.
Lift His name up in the place of His worship and praise today. Amen.
May the Lord bless you in Jesus name!

April 20

Good morning Father, Good morning Jesus, Good morning Holy Spirit.

Reading passage
Galatians 6:7-10

Find your watch Word
Galatians 6:8 (Memorise)

Prayer
*The Lord said that as long as He lives, the seed time and harvest will not cease.
Be not deceived whatsoever you sow is what you will reap.
God's word stands and the scripture cannot be broken.
So we should hold fast to doing good. Any good that we do to people will be returned to us.
Think about it and God will minister to you.
Make people happy, do good to them especially people in the house of God. Amen.
May the Lord bless you in Jesus name!*

April 21

Good morning Father, Good morning Jesus, Good morning Holy Spirit.

Reading passage
Galatians 3:13-16

Find your watch Word
Galatians 3:13 (Memorise)

Prayer
*Refuse anything that wants to stand as a curse of the law in your life today.
Sickness, any payment that does not benefit you is not meant for you.
Jesus has been made the curse for you, you are not supposed to nurse any curse like failure, lack, stagnation, poverty, debt and sickness.
Call upon the Lord and refuse them and it shall be well with you in Jesus name. Amen.
May the Lord bless you in Jesus name!*

April 22

Good morning Father, Good morning Jesus, Good morning Holy Spirit.

Reading passage
Psalms 89:28-34

Find your watch Word
Psalms 89:34 (Memorise)

Prayer
The covenant of the Lord always stands. You are the one who needs to be careful of your own covenant.
For example, in verse 28 the Lord promised to keep His covenant and not to break it and verse 31 asks whether you have ever made any promise to God and did not keep it.
Haven't you been lying down even when you're supposed to pray, study your Bible or be present at a meeting, you find it difficult to do?
Try as much as possible to keep your own side of God's covenant and He will help you, you shall prosper. Amen.
May the Lord bless you in Jesus name!

April 23

Good morning Father, Good morning Jesus, Good morning Holy Spirit.

Reading passage
Psalms 119:97

Find your watch Word
Psalms 119:97 (Memorise)

Prayer
Let the law of the Lord (word) be your meditation day and night, this is the only way to be wiser than the enemy.
The word of the Lord is perfect.
Continue to eat it, chant it and sing it every hour.
Ask the Lord for the grace to keep studying and eating the word of God daily. Amen.
May the Lord bless you in Jesus name!

April 24

Good morning Father, Good morning Jesus, Good morning Holy Spirit.

Reading passage
Micah 7:7-9

Find your watch Word
Micah 7:8 (Memorise)

Prayer
Do not be down in your spirit if you have failed, you will definitely rise.
Do not allow Satan to rejoice over you.
He has no right, do not give him place.
Arise and shine again.
Pray on this issue.
You might have fallen or failed, receive the grace to rise again and shine. Amen.
May the Lord bless you in Jesus name!

April 25

Good morning Father, Good morning Jesus, Good morning Holy Spirit.

Reading passage
Psalms 103:2

Find your watch Word
Psalms 103:2 (Memorise)

Prayer
Do not forget all His benefits.
I suppose this day you will sit and think on all the benefits of the Lord in your life.
First and foremost, the Lord made life available for you.
Forget not all His benefits.
Think about your life and count your blessings.
He will fill your mouth with good things. Do you speak good things or bad things?
But the Bible says the Lord fills your mouth with good things.
Start from today to fill your mouth with good things.
Speak good things to yourself and others. Pray for full grace today. Amen.
May the Lord bless you in Jesus name!

April 26

Good morning Father, Good morning Jesus, Good morning Holy Spirit.

Reading passage
Romans 8:1-8

Find your watch Word
Romans 8:6 (Memorise)

Prayer
The law of the Spirit must free you from the law of the flesh.
There is no condemnation for you in Christ Jesus. The Bible says to be carnally minded is death but to be spiritually minded is life and peace.
Pray today that you are of the Spirit and not to death because you are of God.
No condemnation for you.
Confess the word fervently and hold unto it.
God bless you. Amen.
May the Lord bless you in Jesus name!

April 27

Good morning Father, Good morning Jesus, Good morning Holy Spirit.

Reading passage
Leviticus 26:40-42

Find your watch Word
Leviticus 26:42a (Memorise)

Prayer
The Lord respects His covenant to His people. The book of Psalms 89:34, the Lord promised not to break His covenant, nor alter the word that comes out His mouth.
You are a child of covenant.
Remind the Lord of His covenant with you today in your prayers and keep confessing the word of God in Leviticus chapter 26 verse 42a. Amen.
May the Lord bless you in Jesus name!

April 28

Good morning Father, Good morning Jesus, Good morning Holy Spirit.

Reading passage
Acts 10:9-15

Find your watch Word
Acts 10:15b (Memorise)

Prayer
Are you telling God that His word is cleansed or unclean?
Sometimes the Lord talks to you as you feel it, the flesh is a hindrance.
Always live the life of the Spirit and adhere to the instructions of the Lord.
Pray that the Lord will give you a clear hearing of the Spirit so you will not have mistake of identity in the Spirit. Amen.
May the Lord bless you in Jesus name!

April 29

Good morning Father, Good morning Jesus, Good morning Holy Spirit.

Reading passage
Isaiah 42:19-21

Find your watch Word
Isaiah 42: 19-20 (Memorise)

Prayer
Are you a servant of God that sees many things but don't observe them.
Moses saw the burning bush and the Bible recorded that Moses stopped and took time to observe (Exodus 3:2-3).
Always take time to listen and to observe because the Lord communicates with you every minute. The Lord speaks to you in prayers when you read the Bible, but if you are not in the Spirit or take time to search for knowledge and understanding, then you will be one of the deaf God is speaking to in this portion of the scripture. Amen.
May the Lord bless you in Jesus name!

April 30

Good morning Father, Good morning Jesus, Good morning Holy Spirit.

Reading passage
Isaiah 60:19-21

Find your watch Word
Isaiah 60: 19 (Memorise)

Prayer
Prophesy into your life this morning the verse 19 of this reading passage.
The promises of the Lord are ye and Amen.
The scripture says the Lord will be to you an everlasting light.
The light of God will not leave you.
The scripture says the righteous shall shine brighter and brighter until the perfect day.
If the Lord be your light you will never experience darkness in your life.
Receive the grace of strong faith and expectation to this confession. Amen.
May the Lord bless you in Jesus name!

May 1

Good morning Father, Good morning Jesus, Good morning Holy Spirit.

Reading passage
Revelation 3:1-3

Find your watch Word
Revelation 3:2 (Memorise)

Prayer
The voice of the Lord says today be watchful of those things that remain in you that are not yet dead in you.
Call upon God for strength and you will be able to restore them.
God is no respecter of persons.
He is seeking to bring His word to pass in anyone that is ready.
May you find favour in the Lord to help you out from the pit of destruction.
Ask God for grace of rededicating your life to Him.
Tell Him to revive and strengthen you in the journey of life and faith. Amen.
May the Lord bless you in Jesus name!

May 2

Good morning Father, Good morning Jesus, Good morning Holy Spirit.

Reading passage
Hebrews 2:14-18

Find your watch Word
Hebrews 2:16 (Memorise)

Prayer
We are partakers of flesh and blood of Jesus Christ, for this reason we have the grace to be released from every bondage.
The only way we can destroy Satan who has the power of death is through the Communion table that is the flesh and blood of Jesus.
Call upon Jesus Christ and apply His blood. He was tempted and He overcame so He has the power and enablement to deliver those that are tempted. Amen.
May the Lord bless you in Jesus name!

May 3

Good morning Father, Good morning Jesus, Good morning Holy Spirit.

Reading passage
Isaiah 55:10-12

Find your watch Word
Isaiah 55: 11 (Memorise)

Prayer
The word of God and His promises will not return to Him void except it has done those things it was sent for.
Always have the attitude of confessing the word because the Lord said it will not return until it has done what He sent it for.
So if you refuse to say it, you are suffering and limiting yourself.
God will not come and speak it for you. Hold tightly to the word of promise.
It will work for you. Go in prayers and confess the word of God today. Amen.
May the Lord bless you in Jesus name!

May 4

Good morning Father, Good morning Jesus, Good morning Holy Spirit.

Reading passage
2 Corinthians 9:6-9

Find your watch Word
2 Corinthians 9:8 (Memorise)

Prayer
Give as a person who loves God and not a person looking forward to take something from God. The scripture says in verse 8 that God is able to make all grace abound towards you so that you will have sufficiently.
What does God lay upon your heart to give today. May the good God multiply you in all things. Learn to give to others, indirectly you give to God through giving to them. Amen.
May the Lord bless you in Jesus name!

May 5

Good morning Father, Good morning Jesus, Good morning Holy Spirit.

Reading passage
Luke 18:1-5

Find your watch Word
Luke 18:5 (Memorise)

Prayer
The scripture teaches us to pray without giving up. A child of God should learn to pray and not relent in their effort.
God is a God that answers prayer. But when we pray we should pray in faith and have patient to have their desire.
We should remember to put all righteousness in place. Righteousness, self control, patience, humility, meekness, etc.
Think back and rededicate yourself.
Receive the grace to pray and tender your petition to God. Amen.
May the Lord bless you in Jesus name!

May 6

Good morning Father, Good morning Jesus, Good morning Holy Spirit.

Reading passage
Romans 8:5-8

Find your watch Word
Romans 8:8 (Memorise)

Prayer
If you are in the flesh, it is impossible to please God in the Spirit.
Walk with God in the Spirit. The Lord wants us to have total victory and with this our joy will be complete.
Flesh work with fear and fear is of Satan.
You cannot please the world and please God.
Check yourself because you cannot have a spring of water bringing forth both cold and hot.
It is impossible. The same mouth you use to pray cannot swear or curse and speak all dirty worldly talks. You have to choose who to serve today (Joshua 24:14-15).
Serve the Lord in purity and sincerity.
Ask the Lord to help you so that you will fulfil destiny. Amen.
May the Lord bless you in Jesus name!

May 7

Good morning Father, Good morning Jesus, Good morning Holy Spirit.

Reading passage
Psalms 20:1-3

Find your watch Word
Psalms 2:1 (Memorise)

Prayer
*The Lord is the helper of the helpless.
He is the only one that can help in times of trouble. Man cannot deliver you, the only person that can is the Lord.
The scripture says the Lord will send you help from His Sanctuary and strengthen you.
He sent Angels on behalf of Hezekiah against Sennacherib and the enemies were all dead.
Pray and tell the Lord to send you help.
Take His word to Him. Amen.
May the Lord bless you in Jesus name!*

May 8

Good morning Father, Good morning Jesus, Good morning Holy Spirit.

Reading passage
Ephesians 5:11-14

Find your watch Word
Ephesians 5:15 (Memorise)

Prayer
The Bible wants us to rebuke every work that has to do with darkness.
The Lord Himself wants us to redeem the time for the days are evil.
We need to adhere to all these as a child of light.
Evil is multiplying daily in the world and Satan is so wicked and would not take it lightly with anyone that belongs to Christ.
The Lord will enlighten the eye of your understanding.
Pray the grace of enlightenment and guidance.
The Lord of peace will help you.
You cannot afford to be careless in the battle field.
Amen.
May the Lord bless you in Jesus name!

May 9

Good morning Father, Good morning Jesus, Good morning Holy Spirit.

Reading passage
1 Corinthians 4:17-20

Find your watch Word
1 Corinthians 4:20 (Memorise)

Prayer
*The kingdom of God is not in words but in power.
We should always bear this in mind.
We are the fruit we carry power.
God wants us to be identified with His greatness and lordship.
The child of a king always carries the presence and identity of his Father.
Pray for grace that the power of God be reflected in all you do. Amen.
May the Lord bless you in Jesus name!*

May 10

Good morning Father, Good morning Jesus, Good morning Holy Spirit.

Reading passage
Hebrews 12:14-15

Find your watch Word
Hebrews 12:14 (Memorise)

Prayer
We are the light of the world and salt as well according to the scripture.
If the salt loses its flavour, the value is gone (Matthew 5:13).
We need to bear fruit after the order of our heavenly Father.
The Lord will give you the understanding to live a life void of bitterness and the peace of God will overwhelm you.
Pray and prophesy into your life. Amen.
May the Lord bless you in Jesus name!

May 11

Good morning Father, Good morning Jesus, Good morning Holy Spirit.

Reading passage
Isaiah 53:3-5

Find your watch Word
Isaiah 53:5 (Memorise)

Prayer
Jesus Christ, the scripture says was made a curse for us to receive the Abrahamic blessing. He was also bruised for our transgression; the chastisement of our peace was upon Him and by His stripes we are healed.

You must ponder on all these afflictions Jesus Christ went through for our sake. Rise up for your deliverance.

The Lord is able to deliver us. Psalms 91:15a says "I will deliver you in time of trouble." Let the Lord arise and fight your battle you can do it.

Receive the grace to pray today. Amen.
May the Lord bless you in Jesus name!

May 12

Good morning Father, Good morning Jesus, Good morning Holy Spirit.

Reading passage
Ephesians 6:1-3

Find your watch Word
Ephesians 6:3 (Memorise)

Prayer
The law of God is not grievous, you need to obey the Lord.
He has commanded you to obey your Father in the Lord.
Honour your father and your mother for you to live long.
Always remember obedience is better than sacrifice and God always honours His word. The testimony of God is right.
He is a just God. He will never fail.
The Lord said He respects His covenant.
A child of covenant does not disobey.
God will give you the wisdom to consider the words of God and obey it. Amen.
May the Lord bless you in Jesus name!

May 13

Good morning Father, Good morning Jesus, Good morning Holy Spirit.

Reading passage
Psalms 107:12-21

Find your watch Word
Psalms 107:22 (Memorise)

Prayer
*The Lord wants our offering of thanksgiving.
We should have the knowledge of all these.
God is God and He is unique in our case.
The best way to please God is by giving consistence thanksgiving offering.
If we do not reference the Lord for all He has done for us, we cannot receive more.
God also wants us to give thanks with joy.
Use this time to give total praise and thanksgiving to the Lord. Amen.
May the Lord bless you in Jesus name!*

May 14

Good morning Father, Good morning Jesus, Good morning Holy Spirit.

Reading passage
Psalms 63:2-7

Reading passage
Psalms 63:7 (Memorise)

Prayer
Do you meditate upon God's word that you read or hear every day?
If not, from now, you need to remember God when you sit or lie down and meditate on His goodness and loving kindness.
He is faithful that called us, who will also do it.
Amen.
May the Lord bless you in Jesus name!

May 15

Good morning Father, Good morning Jesus, Good morning Holy Spirit.

Reading passage
Psalms 102:13-15

Find your watch Word
Psalms 102:13 (Memorise)

Prayer
The Lord to favour you today because it is your turn to shine; it is your era and the Lord will bless and compass you about with His favour.
The Lord is near; the Bible says call upon Him and engage your Angels to run errands for you. Your Father is always available because you are destined for favour. Amen.
May the Lord bless you in Jesus name!

May 16

Good morning Father, Good morning Jesus, Good morning Holy Spirit.

Reading passage
Hebrews 4:13-16

Find your watch Word
Hebrews 4:16 (Memorise)

Prayer
The Lord knows all things that we pass through. The scripture says that we do not have a High Priest who cannot sympathise with our weaknesses.
We have the boldness to go to Him at any time to receive grace at the throne.
Do not be discouraged; call your Father at any time to tell Him your need. He does know your concern but He wants you tell Him as a Father. God wants to act on your behalf but He needs you to tell Him.
Speak to Him this morning to receive answer to your desires. Amen.
May the Lord bless you in Jesus name!

May 17

Good morning Father, Good morning Jesus, Good morning Holy Spirit.

Reading passage
Colossians 2:6-8

Find your watch Word
Colossians 2:7 (Memorise)

Prayer
Be rooted in the Lord.
How can you do this?
You should be close to your Bible everyday and every time. God wants us to think about Him, His kingdom, all about Him.
When you always do the things of the world, you tend to think about flesh.
Diving into the things of God is doing the things of the Spirit.
Read the scripture, pray for other people, love and give to the work of God.
I pray God will visit you today in Jesus name.
You will be rooted in Him. Amen.
May the Lord bless you in Jesus name!

May 18

Good morning Father, Good morning Jesus, Good morning Holy Spirit.

Reading passage
Hebrews 4:13-16

Find your watch Word
Hebrews 4:15 (Memorise)

Prayer
Jesus Christ has passed through temptations and He held tightly to His confession commanding the words of God for victory.
He overcame the wicked one. Whatsoever we are passing through is not strange.
Hold tightly to the word of the scripture and be patient until your victory comes. Let us attend to the throne of grace to obtain mercy with boldness. Jesus Christ is Lord.
He carried curses for us that we might have the blessing of Abraham through faith.
Glory to God. Amen. Go to your prayer alter and raise up your voice with boldness.
You are victorious, pour out your heart to Him.
Amen.
May the Lord bless you in Jesus name!

May 19

Good morning Father, Good morning Jesus, Good morning Holy Spirit.

Reading passage
Luke 11:1-4

Find your watch Word
Luke 11:4 (Memorise)

Prayer
When you pray search your heart. If there is anyone you have not forgiven then find your watch Word today its the forgiveness of sin. Jesus wants us to forgive who hurt us at one time or the other that our prayers may be effective. God wants you well but the standard of God should be put into consideration. Every blessing of God is underpinned by standard and rules; none of it is free. Amen. May the Lord bless you in Jesus name!

May 20

Good morning Father, Good morning Jesus, Good morning Holy Spirit.

Reading passage
1 Corinthians 6:5-9

Find your watch Word
1 Corinthians 6:9 (Memorise)

Prayer
Be not deceived; God is no respecter of any man. The unrighteous will not inherit the kingdom of God.

If you read from verse 5, the scripture tells us that it is not good to take ourselves to the law court. It actually said that it is better to accept fault or be cheated than for you to go to court.

If the Lord said anyone who does this will not enter His kingdom, how much more adulterers, fornicators, etc.

Our God is a just God, whatever you sow, that you will reap. Learn to move debris from your way to eternal life. Amen.

May the Lord bless you in Jesus name!

May 21

Good morning Father, Good morning Jesus, Good morning Holy Spirit.

Reading passage
John 3:27, 30-31

Find your watch Word
John 3:31 (Memorise)

Prayer
The scripture says nobody can receive anything except it is given from above.
Again, the Bible says that he who came from above is above all. Jesus Christ is the one that came from above and the Holy Spirit.
The Trinity is one, so no man has been in the heart and can claim to have come from above except with faith. Join your faith with Christ and you can tell the devil you are from above.
You are joint heirs with Christ; you have the right to claim your inheritance in Christ and your possession as well.
Open your mouth this morning and claim them all. Amen.
May the Lord bless you in Jesus name!

May 22

Good morning Father, Good morning Jesus, Good morning Holy Spirit.

Reading passage
1 John 5:1-5

Find your watch Word
1 John 5:5 (Memorise)

Prayer
This is a wonderful promise.
The scripture says, he who believes that Jesus is the son of God overcomes the world.
I am always happy whenever I remember I overcame the world.
You can enter into this promise and speak and claim your inheritance.
Nobody should deceive you that they can pray for you.
You must pray with the word and promises of God to get to the supernatural on this platform.
The Lord reaches unto His children.
Key into God's promises today to receive from Him. Amen.
May the Lord bless you in Jesus name!

May 23

Good morning Father, Good morning Jesus, Good morning Holy Spirit.

Reading passage
Psalms 35:9-11

Find your watch Word
Psalms 35:10a (Memorise)

Prayer
The Lord is teaching us today that He is the only deliverer.
God has thousand ways to deliver His people.
All you need do is to rely on Him, tell Him you are in His hands.
The scripture says He will deliver you from him who is too strong for you.
Leave all those difficult issues into His hands.
He is the Master of the universe, nobody can question Him why He did A or B.
The Lord is just. Amen.
May the Lord bless you in Jesus name!

May 24

Good morning Father, Good morning Jesus, Good morning Holy Spirit.

Reading passage
1 John 5:13-15

Find your watch Word
1 John 5:14a (Memorise)

Prayer
The confidence you have is that if you ask anything according to God's will in Jesus name, He is able to do it for you.
Psalms 37:5 tells us to commit everything unto the Lord, and to trust in Him.
He is able to do it. You are the authority over every situation of the world when the finished the creation, He created man last and asked him to dominate.
Start the work of dominion, trust God. Amen.
May the Lord bless you in Jesus name!

May 25

Good morning, Good morning Jesus, Good morning Holy Spirit.

Reading passage
Colossians 2:6-10

Find your watch Word
Colossians 2:10 (Memorise)

Prayer
The Lord Jesus in the scripture is the head of all principalities and power; you must therefore be rooted in Christ. How?
Establish yourself in faith and all you have been taught.
Put on the whole armour of God, Jesus Christ the superior; put your trust and confidence in Him. No other authority. He is the head of all principalities, power and dominion.
You are seated with Him in heavenly places. Call upon Him and give thanks because He always hears us. Amen.
May the Lord bless you in Jesus name!

May 26

Good morning Father, Good morning Jesus, Good morning Holy Spirit.

Reading passage
2 Timothy 1:8-12

Find your watch Word
2 Timothy 1:12 (Memorise)

Prayer
Are you sure that God is able to keep whatever you keep in His care to the end?
He's a wonderful God. If you can hold tightly to the plan of God for your life, be patient and acknowledge God always.
He is able to carry you through. Commit your way unto the Lord and He will bring it to pass open your mouth and tell the devil you are above Him because you are seated with Jesus in heavenly places. Take your inheritance. Amen.
May the Lord bless you in Jesus name!

May 27

Good morning Father, Good morning Jesus, Good morning Holy Spirit.

Reading passage
1 Corinthians 2:10-12

Find your watch Word
1 Corinthians 2:12 (Memorise)

Prayer
The scripture tells of the strength and the power of the Spirit of God.
It's the Spirit of God that searches the things of God and man. This does not matter.
I still felt we needed the Spirit of God to direct us in all things.
You can see how important the Spirit of God is. The Spirit is a helper who made you to get to places in life.
Desire to have this Spirit; pray in the Spirit for insight as it pertains to the things of the flesh and/or the Spirit. Amen.
May the Lord bless you in Jesus name!

May 28

Good morning Father, Good morning Jesus, Good morning Holy Spirit.

Reading passage
Colossians 2:13-15

Find your watch Word
Colossians 2:15 (Memorise)

Prayer
For God so loved the world and He gave Jesus to you.
He brought us to light and fullness of life through which we became dead to sin.
Jesus nailed our sin with Himself on the cross and everything that is contrary to His purpose for us.
We were made to triumph over principalities, power and dominion.
What I am saying is, you are free. Jesus Christ has been made a curse for your sake.
Take your freedom pass today in prayers. Amen.
May the Lord bless you in Jesus name!

May 29

Good morning Father, Good morning Jesus, Good morning Holy Spirit.

Reading passage
1 John 3:21-24

Find your watch Word
1 John 3:23 (Memorise)

Prayer
If we keep the commandment of God. He will hear our prayers.
The confidence we have is that we belong to Him when we keep His commandment and love one another.
Let us do a check of our lives. Are we in love and are we keeping His commandments?
Go into prayer of rededication this morning to say "Father have mercy and forgive me all my sins."
Amen.
May the Lord bless you in Jesus name!

May 30

Good morning Father, Good morning Jesus, Good morning Holy Spirit.

Reading passage
Proverbs 15:29-33

Find your watch Word
Proverbs 15:33 (Memorise)

Prayer
The fear of the Lord is an instruction of wisdom.
The Lord resists the proud and promotes the humble.
Anything that is different to the fear of God has to do with pride.
Do you fear the Lord? It is written that if you love the Lord you will keep His commandments. My brothers and sisters the Spirit wants us to check our relationship with others.
Are you pretending to be a Christian?
The Bible says you cannot deceive God.
Whatsoever a man sows that will he reap.
Ask God for the spirit of humility and love today.
Amen.
May the Lord bless you in Jesus name!

May 31

Good morning Father, Good morning Jesus, Good morning Holy Spirit.

Reading passage
Ephesians 3:10-20

Find your watch Word
Ephesians 3: 20 (Memorise)

Prayer
God is unique and able to do exceedingly and abundantly more than we ask of Him. Jesus is the centre of our riches in the whole earth. He is our confidence.

The scripture says we are seated with Him in heavenly places far above all principalities and powers and dominion.

There is no mountain that is higher than Him alone. The families in heaven and earth were named after Him. Again, the scripture says we are strengthened by Him in our inner man.

What are you passing through at the moment? Jesus had paid for all, He will help you and strengthen you from Zion. Isaiah 41:10, says "I will help you, fear not, be not dismayed I will help and hold you with my righteous hands".

Speak today with the scriptures, tell Him to help you. He's beside you, able to do exceedingly abundantly. Amen.

May the Lord bless you in Jesus name!

June 1

Good morning Father, Good morning Jesus, Good morning Holy Spirit.

Reading passage
Matthew 13:50-56

Find your watch Word
Matthew 13:54b; Mark 6:2 (Memorise)

Prayer
What do you know Jesus Christ to be: The child of a carpenter and Mary or a Saviour?
The wisdom of God is very essential for a born again child of God.
You need the type of wisdom Jesus displayed in this passage but yet some think is a child of a carpenter to relegate His glory.
But you cannot relegate God. The foolishness of God is better than the wisdom of man.
Seek the face of the Lord through the name of Jesus and desire the type of wisdom Jesus had.
Amen.
May the Lord bless you in Jesus name!

June 2

Good morning Father, Good morning Jesus, Good morning Holy Spirit.

Reading passage
Ecclesiastes 12: 1 – 4

Find your watch Word
Ecclesiastes 12:1 (Memorise)

Prayer
Remember your creator in the days of your youth, listen to the words of God, study the Bible, and involve yourself with the things of the Spirit.
It cannot be done by flesh but in the spirit.
You are too young to ignore the Lord because you have a long way to go.
I want you to ask the Lord to give you the grace to know Him now because your future will be easy with the knowledge of God. Amen.
May the Lord bless you in Jesus name!

June 3

Good morning, Good morning Jesus, Good morning Holy Spirit.

Reading passage
1 Corinthians 2: 6 -10

Find your watch Word
1 Corinthians 2:9 (Memorise)

Prayers
The wisdom of God can be discussed or taught among the matured Christian.
This is because it's always in parables and it contains the mystery of God.
So it may not be straight forward or meaningful when you read it.
It needs people to digest it and know what the Lord is saying.
The scripture says "eyes have not seen, ears have not heard or is it gone into the hearts of men what the Lord has for his children."
God wants to give you this wisdom.
Pray for the type of grace this morning for God to make it available to you. Amen.
May the Lord bless you in Jesus name!

June 4

Good morning Father, Good morning Jesus, Good morning Holy Spirit.

Reading passage
Isaiah 24: 1- 12

Find your watch Word
Isaiah 24:12 (Memorise)

Prayer
The Earth has been cursed because of the activities of Satan on earth.
The scripture said the whole earth is languishing and defiled.
Those on the Earth are desolate and burned and few men are left.
What do you think is left to be trusted in the earth except Christ, as the scripture says only few men are left?
Are you among the few left?
Search your heart today and make a change.
Make a change in your stand with God and start a new live looking unto Jesus and ask Him for the help of the Holy Spirit. Amen.
May the Lord bless you in Jesus name!

June 5

Good morning Father, Good morning Jesus, Good morning Holy Spirit.

Reading passage
Proverbs 24: 4-7

Find your watch Word
Proverbs 24:4-5 (Memorise)

Prayer
The book of Proverbs has given the characteristics of a wise man. Are you wise?
Do you say all your plan and counsel to the whole world and family so they can monitor your life? Verse 7 confirmed it. Increase in wisdom and understanding.
You cannot plan your life by your worldly wisdom because the book of James 3:15 described it as sensual, earthly, demonic wisdom.
Seek the wisdom of God that comes from above.
Amen.
May the Lord bless you in Jesus name!

June 6

Good morning Father, Good morning Jesus, Good morning Holy Spirit

Reading passage
Ephesians 3:20 – 21

Find your watch Word
Ephesians 3:20 (Memorise)

Prayer
The Lord is able to do more exceedingly, abundantly more than you can ask of Him.
We should continue to ask and not allow Satan to close our mouth.
The Father commanded us to ask until our joy is full.
God has given us the responsibility to ask Him whatever we desire Him to do.
When we are on the road, at work or at home we should ask whatever we desire from Him.
Prayer should be without ceasing (1 Thessalonians 5:17). Amen.
May the Lord bless you in Jesus name!

June 7

Good morning Father, Good morning Jesus, Good morning Holy Spirit

Reading passage
Daniel 9:1-5

Find your watch Word
Daniel 9:3 (Memorise)

Prayer
Daniel got his wisdom and understanding from reading. Children of God can generate their knowledge and understanding from reading. Read the Bible always and spiritually inspired books written by men and women of God. The plan of God for us is to live in wisdom and dominion.
The earth is the Lord's and everything there in. The scripture says the earth shall be filled with the glory of God as the waters cover the sea. You have to develop the attitude of reading. So ask the Lord to help you today to develop the spirit of studying and to destroy laziness. He is a faithful God, He will do it. Amen. May the Lord bless you in Jesus name!

June 8

Good morning Father, Good morning Jesus, Good morning Holy Spirit

Reading passage
Daniel 1:8-17

Find your watch Word
Daniel 1:15 (Memorise)

Prayer
The Lord remains faithful, let the whole earth be liars.
Daniel trusted the Lord to death.
He purposed in his heart as a child of God not to defile himself with the king's food.
God is just and able God.
Daniel and others refused the king's food and they remained better than those who were fed by the king.
Do not love life too much, (Revelation 12:11).
Amen.
May the Lord bless you in Jesus name!

June 9

Good morning Father, Good morning Jesus, Good morning Holy Spirit

Reading passage
Proverbs 24:30–34

Find your watch Word
Proverbs 24:30 (Memorise)

Prayer
Laziness is a disease.
The Lord Himself is not lazy neither does He want His children to be lazy.
A lazy hand the devil keeps busy.
A child of God has to be diligent in all he or she does.
Our God wants us to be diligent and faithful.
Anything different to that is lacking understanding.
We are created to have wisdom, understanding and counsel of God.
Children of God should be for excellence and not misfortune.
Do not be lazy.
Pray for the grace to be up and about doing the spiritual and physical work. Amen.
May the Lord bless you in Jesus name!

June 10

Good morning Father, Good morning Jesus, Good morning Holy Spirit

Reading passage
Isaiah 64:1-3

Find your watch Word
Isaiah 64:1 (Memorise)

Prayer
Lord rend the heaven because of my case. Show yourself strong on my side.
Let the mountain shake at your presence concerning my adversaries.
I am looking up to you, my eyes are on you; help me Lord.
Ask the Lord for grace; call upon Him today.
I prevail in all my afflictions in the name of Jesus.
Amen.
May the Lord bless you in Jesus name!

June 11

Good morning Father, Good morning Jesus, Good morning Holy Spirit

Reading passage
James 3:13-18

Find your watch Word
James 3:17 (Memorise)

Prayer
There are two types wisdom in operation in the world; the earthly wisdom (or the wisdom of this world) and the wisdom of God.
The scripture says the wisdom of this world is devilish, where there is selfishness, confusion and every evil thing.
The wisdom of this world is demonic.
The scripture said that the fruit of righteousness is sown by those who make peace.
Are you one of those?
You can desire it today. Amen.
May the Lord bless you in Jesus name!

June 12

Good morning Father, Good morning Jesus, Good morning Holy Spirit

Reading passage
2 Timothy 3:13-17

Find your watch Word
2 Timothy 3:14 (Memorise)

Prayer
All scriptures have what it takes to stand for instructions, rebuke, and reproof and instruct in righteousness.
Continue in the truth that you learnt, do not deviate from them and know from whom you have learned them.
The scripture is to keep you pure. Let them be stored in your heart Amen.
Pray for establishment in the truth of the Word of God. Amen.
May the Lord bless you in Jesus name!

June 13

Good morning Father, Good morning Jesus, Good morning Holy Spirit.

Reading passage
2 Peter 2:15-21

Find your watch Word
2 Peter 2:20 (Memorise)

Prayer
For after Jesus had been crucified, we have been given total liberty.
We should not deny or allow ourselves to be entangled with the pollution of the world of sins, fornication, lies, fraudulence, deceits and all sorts of lust that can take us back to the devil.
We need to be open and also remember always the children of whom we are (2 Corinthians 6:13-14). Keep yourself free from all the activities of the wicked. This is a very important area of your Christian living.
Pray always on this not once but always. The Lord of peace will grant you fullness of His wisdom to carry through. Amen.
May the Lord bless you in Jesus name!

June 14

Good morning Father, Good morning Jesus, Good morning Holy Spirit

Reading passage
Psalms 128:1-6

Find your watch Word
Psalms 128:5 (Memorise)

Prayer
We need to fear the Lord in all the things we do.
The blessing of God is put in place for those who fear Him.
You are bound to see and eat the good of the land all the days of your life.
To see the good of Jerusalem is to see the good of the house of the Lord. God bless you.
Lift up your voice and pray today for the good of Jerusalem. Amen.
May the Lord bless you in Jesus name!

June 15

Good morning Father, Good morning Jesus, Good morning, Holly Spirit

Reading passage
Proverbs 8:12-19

Find your watch Word
Proverbs 8:13-14 (Memorise)

Prayer
Pray always for the help of the Holy Spirit to fear the Lord.
This is because nobody can say Jesus is Lord except by the help of the Spirit.
If the Holy Spirit enlightens your eyes of understanding to know that nobody is greater than God, then it will be easy for you to fear Him.
Proverbs 8:15 says that the king can only reign by Him (Jesus).
If the king can only reign by Him, the One who is the Master of the universe, He thus deserves your reference and trust.
The fear of the Lord is the beginning of wisdom (Proverbs 9:10). Amen.
May the Lord bless you in Jesus name!

June 16

Good morning Father, Good morning Jesus, Good morning Holy Spirit

Reading passage
Psalms 89:20-24

Find your watch Word
Psalms 89:22-23 (Memorise)

Prayer
The Lord has made this covenant with you that the child of wickedness shall not overcome you. He also promised to beat down your enemies before you.
I want to encourage you to arise on the platform of this covenant and claim what belongs to you. It's right time for you to rise and pray and take possession of this prophesy.
What you do not confront has the right to stay. Your enemies will not prosper. Amen.
May the Lord bless you in Jesus name!

June 17

Good morning Father, Good morning Jesus, Good morning Holy Spirit

Reading passage
Philippians 4:4-9

Find your watch Word
Philippians 4:6 (Memorise)

Prayer
The Lord said you should be anxious for nothing this morning. Are you anxious?
Do not allow the devil to have his way in your life.
God is able to do all things.
Give thanks for what He has not done.
Many are the afflictions of the righteous but the Lord delivers him out of them all.
God is faithful.
The Bible says in Philippians 4:4 – Rejoice again, I say rejoice. Amen.
May the Lord bless you in Jesus name!

June 18

Good morning Father, Good morning Jesus, Good morning Holy Spirit

Reading passage
1 Timothy 4:1-5

Find your watch Word
1 Timothy 4:2 (Memorise)

Prayer
Be honest and straight forward. The Lord is looking for those who need the fullness of God in their lives without any deceit and hypocrisy. Separate yourself from these ones. God is mindful of those who are all out for Him, those who are not given to the world at all. Satan is watchful of average Christians because they will not exercise themselves with sins. Think out these and start again. Amen. May the Lord bless you in Jesus name!

June 19

Good morning Father, Good morning Jesus, Good morning Holy Spirit

Reading passage
Proverbs 19:16–17

Find your watch Word
Proverbs 19:16 (Memorise)

Prayer
The scripture teaches us not to be careless. What does this mean? It means wisdom, sensitivity to the things that are necessary like understanding, knowledge, etc. An adage says stitch in time saves nine.
If we are wise in all we do, praying for every step we take in life, we will not miss our ways. Take directions from God and not putting our trust in man.
Those who put God aside and put their trust in man, the Lord has cursed them already. He says they will not see good.
Pray for God's help and grace today not to be careless in life. Amen.
May the Lord bless you in Jesus name!

June 20

Good morning Father, Good morning Jesus, Good morning Holy Spirit

Reading passage
Proverbs 19:1-9

Find your watch Word
Proverbs 19:5,9 (Memorise)

Prayer
The Scripture commanded us not to be a false witness.
Do you perverse your lips, the punishment is at the door.
Integrity is for the child of God, if you keep commandment of God.
He that keeps the commandment keeps his soul. Amen.
May the Lord bless you in Jesus name!

June 21

Good morning Father, Good morning Jesus, Good morning Holy Spirit

Reading passage
Proverbs 19:20-21

Find your watch Word
Proverbs 19:20

Prayer
Counsel and instruction are very much alike. The scripture this morning encourages you to listen to counsel and receive instructions. Invariably this is telling you that you cannot know all and everything.
We have diverse instructions from God and from people of God.
The parents themselves have instructions for their children.
Do you listen to counsel and obey instruction from both God and your biological parents?
I implore you by the special grace of God to consult the Lord always and listen to your parents, both biological and spiritual parents, (Ephesians 6:1-2). God wants you to do these things so that you might live long. Pray on these things this morning. God bless you. Amen.
May the Lord bless you in Jesus name!

June 22

Good morning Father, Good morning Jesus, Good morning Holy Spirit

Reading passage
Proverbs 4:18-19

Find your watch Word
Proverbs 4:18 (Memorise)

Prayer
*The path of the just is like a shining sun that shines until the perfect day.
We should be holy like our Father in heaven, is a command of the Lord.
Everything that is still not giving us the clear path of the just should be removed.
He is the Lord and He does not change.
We should continue to pray until our joy is full.*

June 23

Good morning Father, Good morning Jesus, Good morning Holy Spirit

Reading passage
Proverbs 2: 4-6

Find your watch Word
Proverbs 2:6 (Memorise)

Prayer
It is a good thing to search for the Lord Jesus Christ. The book of Proverbs chapter 2 tells us that Jesus Christ must be searched for as silver and gold and as hidden treasure.

This means you need to consistently search in prayers, reading of Christian books and the scripture.

The Lord grants us the grace to continue our race without any hindrance.

Remember to '... seek first the kingdom of God and its righteousness and all ... things shall be added unto you' – Matthew 6:33.

Let the Spirit teach you how to pray this morning. Amen.

May the Lord bless you in Jesus name!

June 24

Good morning Father, Good morning Jesus, Good morning Holy Spirit

Reading passage
Revelation 5:11-13

Find your watch Word
Revelation 5:12 (Memorise)

Prayer
*You need to think about how the heaven and the earth are worshipping the Lord.
If there is nothing different in Him the earth and heaven will not be worshipping Him.
Read verse 12 follow on to pray and ask the Lord to give you insight on the largeness of God.
You need a large heart to know your God is powerful, honourable and glorious.
Pray for insight and understanding. Amen.
May the Lord bless you in Jesus name!*

June 25

Good morning Father, Good morning Jesus, Good morning Holy Spirit

Reading passage
Ecclesiastes 7:18-19

Find your watch Word
Ecclesiastes 7:19 (Memorise)

Prayer
Wisdom, the scripture says is stronger than the ruler of a city.
When you have wisdom you are free. God is the giver of this wisdom; it is not of the world. The scripture in the book of James 1:17 says "Every good and perfect gift comes from the Father of light above."
Pray today that the giver of wisdom will give you and you shall not miss it in life. Amen.
May the Lord bless you in Jesus name!

June 26

Good morning Father, Good morning Jesus, Good morning Holy Spirit

Reading passage
Job 28:20-24

Find your watch Word
Job 28:20-23 (Memorise)

Prayer
God is looking at the end of the earth because He planned His work already.
Wisdom comes from Him even though we have a worldly wisdom that is of man and devil.
This is because Satan has the fake or counterfeit of every work of God.
Imagine when the Lord sent Moses to Egypt and changed Moses' rod into snake, the magicians of Egypt created fake snake which the Lord's swallowed.
My brothers and sisters put your trust in the Lord that you might find a genuine wisdom from Him.
Amen.
May the Lord bless you in Jesus name!

June 27

Good morning Father, Good morning Jesus, Good morning Holy Spirit

Reading passage
Luke 11:49-52

Find your watch Word
Proverbs 19:21 (Memorise)

Prayer
Jesus Christ is the wisdom of God and the scripture says that the earth may pass away, but not an iota of the Word of God will pass away unfulfilled.
The Find your watch Word in Proverb 19:21 says the counsel of God shall stand.
The counsel of God is the Word of God. Your wisdom is Christ Jesus.
Hold on to His Word today because Jesus is the "Word".
Use the Word to pray in your desire. Amen.
May the Lord bless you in Jesus name!

June 28

Good morning Father, Good morning Jesus, Good morning Holy Spirit

Reading passage
John 4:7-9

Find your watch Word
1 John 4:8 (Memorise)

Prayer
The love of God for mankind cannot be fathomed. God never jokes about the type of love He commands us to have. God is no respecter of anyone when it comes to obeying His commandment.

We must be careful because we might have the whole world but if we fail to keep God's commandment, we are on our own.

Always make sure that you are on His side in everything. Love your neighbour as the Lord is a very strong love, it is because prayers cannot be answered when love is locked out of prayer.

Repent this morning and let go of any offense against anybody for God to hear and answer your prayer.

God bless you as you pray today. Amen. May the Lord bless you in Jesus name!

June 29

Good morning Father, Good Morning Jesus, Good morning Holy Spirit

Reading passage
John 17:20-23

Find your watch Word
John 17:21 (Memorise)

Prayer
Always remember that you should be united with God. The Spirit of oneness is very important. The Lord said if two shall come together and ask anything in His name, it shall be done for them. The Lord will surround you with the Spirit of oneness.
The Trinity is one, which is why we see things done every month.
The understanding of this will not elude you. Pray for grace and the Lord will surprise you. Amen. May the Lord bless you in Jesus name!

June 30

Good morning Father, Good morning Jesus, Good morning Holy Spirit

Reading passage
1 Timothy 4:9-16

Find your watch Word
1Timothy 4:12 (Memorise)

Prayer
Do not allow anybody to mock your youth. Strive to be a good example to all other youths.
Be a good example in word, in conduct and in love.
The scripture says that God puts love on top of other laws and the scripture says we are the 'book' that other people read.
Whatsoever you are in words or in your relationships or behaviour will move people more, than your preaching to them from the Bible.
We have to contain ourselves; godliness in all our actions thoughts and love to the world.
Satan enters into our life to deliver curses when we are not pure in all these opening love, words and conduct.
If our lives are right, then our listening will be smooth and envious. Pray for the grace, wisdom and enablement Spirit. Amen.
May the Lord bless you in Jesus name!

July 1

Good morning Father, Good morning Jesus, Good morning Holy Spirit

Reading passage
1 Timothy 3:14-16

Find your watch Word
1 Timothy 3:15 (Memorise)

Prayer
Paul's directive in this part of the scripture is that we should know how to conduct ourselves in the house of God.
This is the continuation of what we learnt yesterday, in verse 15 of the portion of scripture. What is your own conduct to the saints in the Church of God?
God wants you to take the weight and checks. Do you backbite or condemn people? Are you pure or perfect in all your ways? Lift up your voice this morning.
I am persuaded the Holy Spirit has taken over, let Him help your cleansing this morning. Amen. May the Lord bless you in Jesus name!

July 2

Good morning Father, Good morning Jesus, Good morning Holy Spirit

Reading passage
Jeremiah 1:17-19

Find your watch Word
Jeremiah 1:19 (Memorise)

Prayer
The Lord has foreseen the stages of your life before your parents gave birth to you.
The world is a battle front; no man on earth escapes the battles of life, you have to fight them.
The scriptures give us hope in Christ Jesus because we have the assurance in God that they will fight with us but will not overcome or prevail against.
Whatever battles you are facing, draw closer to God and study the Word of God.
Use the Word of God in your prayers to fight the battles. If Jesus Christ could prevail, you will prevail. Amen.
May the Lord bless you in Jesus name!

July 3

Good morning Father, Good morning Jesus, Good morning Holy Spirit

Reading passage
Lamentations 3:31-33

Find your watch Word
Lamentations 3:33 (Memorise)

Prayer
I do not know why the Lord chooses to speak to you this morning like this, this week.
He could feel our pains and anguish.
Consider verse 33 of this passage.
Jesus Christ gave Himself for us long ago when He shed His own blood.
The BLOOD OF JESUS IS ENOUGH for you in whatever situation.
He will not cast us off forever.
He will show us compassion.
Take time to study this chapter 3 of Lamentations.
God wants us to wait patiently for Him.
I declare today He will surprise you.
Worship Him this morning and minister to God in your songs. Amen.
May the Lord bless you in Jesus name!

July 4

Good morning Father, Good morning Jesus, Good morning Holy Spirit

Reading passage
Galatians 3:13-14

Find your watch Word
Galatians 3:15b (Memorise)

Prayer
Here the scripture talks about the seed of Abraham, which is the promise of God to us.
The law cannot annul the covenant of God for you or make it of no effect.
This means that we cannot be cursed because Jesus Christ had gone for us.
You have to continue to pronounce the promise and the covenant every time to destroy the attack of Satan in any area of your life.
Jesus Christ had been made a curse that the promise of Abraham might get into your hand.
Claim the blessing of Abraham today, it's all yours.
Jesus Christ had gone ahead of you. Amen.
May the Lord bless you in Jesus name!

July 5

Good morning Father, Good morning Jesus, Good morning Holy Spirit

Reading passage
1 Corinthians 9:15-26

Find your watch Word
1 Corinthians 9:22 (Memorise)

Prayer
What are you doing to bring someone into the kingdom of God?
Are you preaching the Gospel?
The scripture tells us how important it is for us to win souls into the kingdom of God.
This is one of the things that moves the Lord and makes Him happy.
1 Corinthians 9:22 says "I became weak to the weak."
Think of what to do today to make God happy and think about you.
Let God speak to you when you give Him time to tell you what to do to move Him about the souls that needed to be saved through you. Amen.
May the Lord bless you in Jesus name!

July 6

Good morning Father, Good morning Jesus, Good morning Holy Spirit

Reading passage
Philippians 1:27-30

Find your watch Word
Philippians 1:27a (Memorise)

Prayer
Let your conduct be stable as that of Christ, so that your faith will stand.
If whatever you are doing is for God, in your understanding, then you will have joy, and victory will always attend to you.
You are partakers of Jesus' suffering so let your trust in Christ be stable as all things will work to your good.
Whether the Pastor is there or not, Jesus is always there for you.
Pray for the grace to stand. Amen.
May the Lord bless you in Jesus name!

July 7

Good morning Father, Good morning Jesus, Good morning Holy Spirit.

Reading passage
Proverbs 13:20

Find your watch Word
Proverbs 13:20 (Memorise)

Prayer
The scripture this morning is searching your heart. He who walks with the wise will be wise. Are you walking with the wise, does your conscience check you against the type of group you associate with?
The Lord wants you to check your whole life with the set of people you move with. Have a change of heart today.
Consider verse 20b which says the communion of fools will be destroyed.
The scripture cannot be broken. The Lord will remain Lord forever.
Pray for the grace to relate with your present group.
Ask the Lord for the opportunity to share the Gospel with them and to lead them to Christ or if need be to break away from them. Amen.
May the Lord bless you in Jesus name!

July 8

Good morning Father, Good morning Jesus, Good morning Holy Spirit

Reading passage
Joshua 1:10-11

Find your watch Word
Joshua 1:11 (Memorise)

Prayer
Joshua set time frame for himself in this task of crossing the Jordan.
In whatsoever you do, set a time frame for yourself and ensure that you achieve something good out of it.
Do not put too much in at a time and waste years.
God wants children that put time frame and achieve it.
Call upon God for wisdom of time frame and achievement today. Amen.
May the Lord bless you in Jesus name!

July 9

Good morning Father, Good morning Jesus, Good morning Holy Spirit.

Reading passage
Joshua 2:1-2

Find your watch Word
Joshua 2:1 (Memorise)

Prayer
Focus on those things that bring result.
Always live your life with strategies.
Always focus on those things that work for you.
Choose leaders that reflect their character.
Joshua knew those two that brought good news and knew that through them good result will come.
Prepare yourself for things that bring result.
Pray for the heart that brings result. Amen.
May the Lord bless you in Jesus name!

July 10

Good morning Father, Good morning Jesus, Good morning Holy Spirit

Reading passage
Joshua 3:13-14

Find your watch Word
Joshua 3:14 (Memorise)

Prayer
*Be careful of fear of mental barrier.
Only hold fast to the promise and the leading of God; that was what helped them cross the Jordan. The Jordan will never move until you step out of it.
Fear has a torment and its the first gift of satan that he uses to decieve any man. You will not be deceived by him.
Let your confidence be consistent.
Do not accept the fear of satan at any point in life. You are covered in Jesus name. Amen.
May the Lord bless you in Jesus name!*

July 11

Good morning Father, Good morning Jesus, Good morning Holy Spirit

Reading passage
Joshua 5:8-9

Find your watch Word
Joshua 5:9 (Memorise)

Prayer
The past was cut off from the life of the children of Israel by way of circumcision.
You cannot have the attitude of the past and go into the future.
Cut off the past attitude and go into the future. Cut off wrong memory of those who despitefully used you, move to the future.
Love them from far off and go your way. Move away nicely.
Circumcision signifies covenant with God and a new beginning; adult hood manna is not meant for the adult, Joshua 5:12.
It is for babies, it's of the past.
Comport yourself. Pray for growth and for the Spirit of maturity. Amen.
May the Lord bless you in Jesus name!

July 12

Good morning Father, Good morning Jesus, Good morning Holy Spirit

Reading passage
Zachariah 8:20-23

Find your watch Word
Zachariah 8:22-23 (Memorise)

Prayer
The Lord said after your prayers had been answered and you have been decorated, people will ask you where your God is.
They want to follow you to the God you serve. You will be a terror to your enemies because they will fear the Lord you serve.
The point I am making is that "OBEDIENCE" is very essential for you.
Live a sinless life and let the Lord lift your head up.
Pray for the grace of sin free life and obedience. Amen.
May the Lord bless you in Jesus name!

July 13

Good morning Father, Good morning Jesus, Good morning Holy Spirit

Reading passage
Deuteronomy 28:1-14

Find your watch Word
Deuteronomy 28:12b (Memorise)

Prayer
You shall lend to many nations.
The book of Deuteronomy is very important for you to read, and in particular Deuteronomy 28:1-14.
God had already spoken your word of blessing and all you need to do is to step into it.
The Find your watch Word says you will lend to many nations.
Do you believe this? Go to God in prayer because the scripture says God puts His Word above His name.
Pray into all around you. You must start to lend to nations. Amen.
May the Lord bless you in Jesus name!

July 14

Good morning Father, Good morning Jesus, Good morning Holy Spirit

Reading passage
Psalms 103:1-8

Find your watch Word
Psalms 103:8 (Memorise)

Prayer
How many times do you bless the Lord in a day?
He is worthy of your praise.
Sometimes you feel like ministering to the Lord of Host.
Just bless Him because that is what He needs from us for other roads to be opened to us.
The verse 8b of our reading passage says God is slow to anger, and abounding in mercy.
We could have been forgotten but for the mercy of God we are sustained.
If you wake up any day, you might feel like blessing Him with your praise, just do it.
Do not ask of anything from Him.
God is faithful, you sleep and rise the second day because He (the Lord) sustains you. Amen.
May the Lord bless you in Jesus name!

July 15

Good morning Father, Good morning Jesus, Good morning Holy Spirit

Reading passage
Psalms 44:1-6

Find your watch Word
Psalms 44:6 (Memorise)

Prayer
Read verse 3 of this passage, what do you think of it? They did not take possession of the land with their own hands or sword.
The verse 6 of this chapter then says, I will not trust in bow nor shall your sword save you.
It is impossible. Turn to God and say the same thing to God.
He is able to deliver us.
The scripture says the outstretched hand of God is mighty.
Look unto Jesus the author and finisher of your faith. Give it to Him, however bad the case may be, He will put it right. Amen.
May the Lord bless you in Jesus name!

July 16

Good morning Father, Good morning Jesus, Good morning Holy Spirit

Reading passage
Psalms 105:37-44

Find your watch Word
Psalms 105:42 (Memorise)

Prayer
The Lord will always remember His holy promise. He said it many times that He will forever remember His covenant, Psalms 105:8.
He wants us to put His laws in our heart and He will do them.
Let your enemies fear you and the Lord you serve. The scripture says the Egyptians were happy that the Israelites departed from them, verse 37b. Pray to God with His Word.
He will remember and honour it in your life. God is God, He does not tell lies.
At the end of every trial in life there is triumph. Cry to the Lord with His Word; He will never forsake you. You will return to thank Him. Amen.
May the Lord bless you in Jesus name!

July 17

Good morning Father, Good morning Jesus, Good morning Holy Spirit

Reading passage
Isaiah 42:9-10

Find your watch Word
Isaiah 42:10a (Memorise)

Prayer
The Word of God is settled in heaven. He promised to do a new thing and He's always sure of His Words. He said "I tell you now before they spring forth". God is very faithful.
He now wants you to sing a new song as well for the new things.
Isaiah 43:18-19, still repeats that God is going to do a new thing.
Your God is the God of new things and new songs. Amen.
May the Lord bless you in Jesus name!

July 18

Good morning Father, Good morning Jesus, Good morning Holy Spirit

Reading passage
1 Peter 1:6

Find your watch Word
Psalms 31:6-9 (Memorise)

Prayer
The test of your faith is real. God wants you to understand that genuineness of your faith is precious to Him.
So it might be tested by fire but found more precious than gold that perishes, it will definitely lead to praise, honour and glory.
This means that though you do not see Him but believe in Him.
When you are tested, you are promoted.
The Lord that you do not see and believe Him will show up to deliver you out of all your troubles.
Amen.
May the Lord bless you in Jesus name!

July 19

Good morning Father, Good morning Jesus, Good morning Holy Spirit

Reading passage
2 Corinthians 4:13-18

Find your watch Word
Ephesians 2:17-18 (Memorise)

Prayer
When you read the Word of God, do you have the same spirit.
If you have the same, you have to start pronouncing the Word of God, prophesy and declare your justification and stand against satan.
Take time to listen to tapes, DVDs of men of God, reading books of men of God, not long you will see your faith rising.
Do you believe what you study and put it in your heart.
The Scripture says you will see far than the physical eyes will see, because your need the things that are not seen which are eternal life to man. Amen.
May the Lord bless you in Jesus name!

July 20

Good morning Father, Good morning Jesus, Good morning Holy Spirit

Reading passage
Ephesians 2:4-10

Find your watch Word
Proverb 4:27 (Memorise)

Prayer
Jesus Christ loves us and in Him there is no disappointment.
When we were yet sinners, the scripture says He died for us.
If you understand Ephesians 2:4-10, Jesus Christ was said to be rich in mercy and love.
If we do not have Jesus, our hope is shattered.
Greater is He who called us and He who called us will also do it.
He will not leave you or forsake you; hold tightly to Him.
The word He gave us is powerful.
Drink it, eat it every day, you will find life and health to your spirit, soul and body. Amen.
May the Lord bless you in Jesus name!

July 21

Good morning Father, Good morning Jesus, Good morning Holy Spirit

Reading passage
1 Peter 1:6-9

Find your watch Word
1 Peter 1:23 (Memorise)

Prayer
*Your faith is precious than gold because it fetches your desire when activated.
So without faith the scripture says you cannot please God.
This is because you are not made of corruptible seed.
Faith is very essential in your daily Christian life.
1 Peter 1:8 says having seen Him, you believe.
Faith is the evidence of things not seen. So you do not see your miracle, but you believe God had done it.
Pray for the grace to build your faith and make it big. Amen.
May the Lord bless you in Jesus name!*

July 22

Good morning Father, Good morning Jesus, Good morning Holy Spirit

Reading passage
Romans 15:26-30

Find your watch Word
Ephesians 2:7 (Memorise)

Prayer
It is good to serve God with all that you have. Be a blessing to the Body of Christ and the whole world.
Do good to others, make somebody laugh, do not make people cry.
Romans 15:26,27 says that the saints in Achaia and Macedonia ministered to the poor saints in Jerusalem with their material and substance.
God will show His exceeding riches to us (Ephesians 2:7).
Pray that God will teach you how to be a blessing.
Amen.
May the Lord bless you in Jesus name!

July 23

Good morning Father, Good morning Jesus, Good morning Holy Spirit

Reading passage
Psalms 105:37-45

Find your watch Word
Psalms 105:42 (Memorise)

Prayer
He remembers His holy promise. The Lord will remember His Holy promise today and make you the pride of nations.
He made the Israelites the pride and envy of their enemies.
Are you ashamed of what the result of your interview will be or your examination? God does not forget His promises.
The scripture says He respects His covenant. He does not break His covenant like man.
Trust in Him and the mercy of God will surround you. Amen.
May the Lord bless you in Jesus name!

July 24

Good morning Father, Good morning Jesus, Good morning Holy Spirit

Reading passage
Isaiah 51:1-3

Find your watch Word
Isaiah 51:3 (Memorise)

Prayer
The Lord has promised who will disannul? Isaiah 51:3 says the Lord is ready to comfort your Zion and its waste places.
He will restore to you all the losses. He will make the wilderness like Eden.
Is that not enough for you to keep your mind at peace?
God remains God when things are changing. Rest your case on Him; He is able to give you your inheritance. Amen.
May the Lord bless you in Jesus name!

July 25

Good morning Father, Good morning Jesus, Good morning Holy Spirit

Reading passage
51:11-16

Find your watch Word
Isaiah 25:8 (Memorise)

Prayer
The Lord will wipe all tears from all faces. There is no reason to cry.
When He promises, He will bring it to fulfilment. Let your peace be stable on the Lord.
He does not waver; the Lord has done it before and He will do it again.
Hallelujah! God is able. Claim your blessings.
Amen.
May the Lord bless you in Jesus name!

July 26

Good morning Father, Good morning Jesus, Good morning Holy Spirit

Reading passage
Psalms 105:17-24

Find your watch Word
Psalms 105:24 (Amen)

Prayer
The Lord has a reason for every of your affliction.
Weeping may endure for a night, but joy comes in the morning.
Joseph was to be destroyed so as to eliminate his dream and vision.
God meant Joseph for good. Isaiah 55:8 says "He was let go free and promoted".
What are those things you are passing through at the moment, the Lord will take you out because He knows of all your pains.
Call upon the name of Jesus and reference His doings in the lives of all our forefathers – Abraham, Isaac, Jacob, Joseph, Noah, David. He can hear you and have a thousand ways when and where it appears there is no way. Amen.
May the Lord bless you in Jesus name!

July 27

Good morning Father, Good morning Jesus, Good morning Holy Spirit

Reading passage
Isaiah 52: 1-3

Find your watch Word
Isaiah 52:1-3 (Memorise)

Prayer
Put on your strength, the Lord says. I want you to put on your garment, this truth, depart from me. He said the uncircumcised, the wicked one will not know your hidden place.
They will not come to you. Shake off yourself from dust. The Lord is your strength.
Glorify the Lord in the power of His Word. There is none like unto Him.
Praise the Lord our redeemer. Amen.
May the Lord bless you in Jesus name!

July 28

Good morning Father, Good morning Jesus, Good morning Holy Spirit

Reading passage
Luke 14:13-23

Find your watch Word
Luke 14:13-14 (Memorise)

Prayer
The reason for you being alive today is to affect lives, to make somebody happy and make them feel comfortable.
But some of God's children tend to put this aside these days. Use your substance to honour the Lord and people that are less able.
God is your source and provider and keeper. Jesus Christ is teaching us the way to consider others in our giving.
Remember some are outside to be brought to the fold. Jesus said if I am lifted up, I will draw people to Myself. If those in the Church refuse to serve God, thousands are outside who do have the knowledge of Christ; they will serve Him. Let us, therefore, go out and tell others about Christ. Use your money and substance to do this.
He will replenish you. Praise God. Receive the grace today. Amen.
May the Lord bless you in Jesus name!

July 29

Good morning Father, Good morning Jesus, Good morning Holy Spirit

Reading passage
Isaiah 25:6-9

Find your watch Word
Isaiah 25:8 (Memorise)

Prayer
*The Lord will destroy the covering and the veil of wickedness from the face of His people.
He will wipe all tears away and the rebuke of His people.
There is no one like unto Him that can deliver.
God is able to deliver you.
He said, with joy will you draw water from the well of salvation.
Ask God to wipe away your tears according to His covenant. Amen.
May the Lord bless you in Jesus name!*

July 30

Good morning Father, Good morning Jesus, Good morning Holy Spirit

Reading passage
Haggai 2:6-7

Find your watch Word
Isaiah 34:8 (Memorise)

Prayer
This is the time of nation shaking. Pray that at this time that vengeance of the Lord comes upon people that it will be your own time of lifting. Walk in the Word and be closer to God, serving the Lord with all your heart. Seek the Lord when He can be found. You will not be a partaker of the present vengeance of God. Amen. May the Lord bless you in Jesus name!

July 31

Good morning Father, Good morning Jesus. Good morning Holy Spirit

Reading passage
Psalms 37:18-19

Find your watch Word
Psalms 5:4 (Memorise)

Prayer
The Lord gave us a covenant of forever inheritance.
He said we shall not be ashamed in evil time and famine.
The Lord is our hope in every situation.
All we need to do is to trust after we have called upon Him. So all we need to do is to call the Lord after we have freed ourselves from sin.
Put your petitions before God today. Amen.
May the Lord bless you in Jesus name!

August 1

Good morning Father, Good morning Jesus, Good morning Holy Spirit

Reading passage
Daniel 2:20-21

Find your watch Word
Psalms 8:1 (Memorise)

Prayer
Pray today that He who is excellent can enthrone and dethrone.
The Bible says He sent His glory upon the earth and heaven. Amen.
May the Lord bless you in Jesus name!

August 2

Good morning Father, Good morning Jesus, Good morning Holy Spirit

Reading passage
James 1:6-8

Find your watch Word
James 1:8 (Memorise)

Prayer
The scripture defines faith as the "substance of things hoped for, the evidence of things not seen" that is already achieved.
Evidence means already achieved. Faith makes the Lord happy and ready to fight a Christian's battle.
Think about your faith level. God does not fail man but man has always been failing Him.
Pray that the Lord will strengthen your faith and increase its level.
He is able to carry you through. Do not remember your past experiences. Amen.
May the Lord bless you in Jesus name!

August 3

Good morning Father, Good morning Jesus, Good morning Holy Spirit

Reading passage
2 Timothy 3:15-16

Find your watch Word
2 Timothy 3:15 (Memorise)

Prayer
*The scripture has to be learnt from childhood.
It is very essential for us to give ourselves to the commandment of God.
Do not forget to read the scripture every day because the Bible lists what it gives us, 2 Timothy 3:16.
If we are lacking any of the listed parts in verse 16, we are likely going to be a failure.
We will not be a failure in Jesus name. Amen.
May the Lord bless you in Jesus name!*

August 4

Good morning Father, Good morning Jesus, Good morning Holy Spirit

Reading passage
Ezekiel 13:19-23

Find your watch Word
Ezekiel 13:23 (Memorise)

Prayer
The Lord is desperate to deliver His people at any point in time.
We should be open to Him and run away from sin to always be fit for His deliverance.
Any stain of sin can take us away from God.
Read the passage very well again and again. Then consider verse 23; it's a word of authority from the throne of grace. "I will deliver my people out of your hand". Go to the throne this morning and request of God for your deliverance. Amen.
May the Lord bless you in Jesus name!

August 5

Good morning Father, Good morning Jesus, Good morning Holy Spirit

Reading passage
Numbers 16:28-30

Find your watch Word
Psalms 121:7 (Memorise)

Prayer
*The children of Israel grieved the Lord because they were rude to Moses.
If we grieve the Holy Spirit, He can be upset and turn away from us.
Another way we can grieve the Lord is through misbehaviour to the Holy Spirit.
Here it was a sin to Moses the servant of God.
May the Lord preserve us.
Pray today to receive God or the Holy Spirit.
Amen.
May the Lord bless you in Jesus name!*

August 6

Good morning Father, Good morning Jesus, Good morning Holy Spirit

Reading passage
Galatians 3:13-14

Find your watch Word
Proverbs 3:33 (Memorise)

Prayer
*Jesus Christ had paid for all that concerns us. So we are redeemed from the curse of the law.
No curse has the right to overtake us.
He did it by His blood. We must always remember that this great price was paid.
The only person cursed is the wicked one.
Read the Find your watch Word again. The just is blessed.
Start by praying in the Spirit today, breaking everything related to curse in your life.
Use the scripture Galatians 3:13-14 and free yourself from curses – Amen.
May the Lord bless you in Jesus name!*

August 7

Good morning Father, Good morning Jesus, Good morning Holy Spirit

Reading passage
2 Corinthians 4:17-18

Find your watch Word
Psalm 121:2 (Memorise)

Prayer
Our life's affliction is for a short time. If we look at the reading passage for today which is talking about present situations which the scripture refers to as affliction.
The only deliverer of our life is Jesus, from whom our help comes.
You can decide to call only on the name of Jesus alone. He is able to carry you and I through.
The book of Psalms refers to Him as our help in times of trouble.
Cry unto Him today, he delivered the Israelites. Psalms 121:1 which says I will lift up my eyes unto the hills......... Call Him. Amen.
May the Lord bless you in Jesus name!

August 8

Good morning Father, Good morning Jesus, Good morning Holy Spirit

Reading passage
Hebrew 12:13-15

Find your watch Word
1 Timothy 6:18 (Memorise)

Prayer
God wants His children to do good. Follow peace with all men.
We have to give ourselves to good works. 1 John 3:18 says we should '... not love in word, neither in tongue, but in deed and in truth'.
Let us search ourselves today as the word of God has been sent to our direction and turn to God so that He will return to us.
He is no respecter of any man. Whatsoever you do to people they will do to you.
Pray today and clear your ground for new season of purity. Amen.
May the Lord bless you in Jesus name!

August 9

Good morning Father, Good morning Jesus, Good morning Holy Spirit.

Reading passage
Luke 2:34-35

Find your watch Word
Colossian 3:25 (Memorise)

Prayer
The birth of Jesus Christ is for the rising and falling of many people. Every man will be judged according to their work. The wrong will receive the reward for the work they have done, likewise the right.

Jesus' birth also was for the liberation of people from all forms of oppression. The right will rise and the wrong may continue to fall or choose to rise. Your prayer this morning is for God to empower you through the birth of Christ Jesus. Secondly, ask that God should make the birth of Christ to set your way to rising and never to fall. Amen.

May the Lord bless you in Jesus name!

August 10

Good morning Father, Good morning Jesus, Good morning Holy Spirit.

Reading passage
2 Kings 2:23-24

Find your watch Word
Ephesians 4:27 (Memorise)

Prayer
Give no place to the devil; always fall to the side of God and let Him instruct you of what to do.
It is right to fall to the side of God which the Scripture says we must not grieve.
If you say anything that is not right to someone even if he's not a man of God, the Spirit of God will take it up.
Be careful on the attitude. Pray for God's instructions and leadings. Amen.
May the Lord bless you in Jesus name!

August 11

Good morning Father, Good morning Jesus, Good morning Holy Spirit.

Reading passage
Zachariah 9:11-12

Find your watch Word
Isaiah 43:26 (Memorise)

Prayer
God called us to plead together with Him. To set us out of the pit where there is no water.
God is set to deliver us and take us out. The will of God in our lives is not farfetched.
The Lord does not want us to be in problem as problems are the will of Satan not the will of God.
Jesus Christ was sent to come and set us free from all those things that the enemies have set on our way as objects of discomfort and enemies of progress.
Pray yourself out of spiritual cages today. Amen.
May the Lord bless you in Jesus name!

August 12

Good morning, Father, Good Jesus, Good morning Holy Spirit.

Reading Passage
Romans 3:25-26

Find your watch Word
1 John 4:10 (Memorise)

Prayer
Jesus Christ had been made sin for us. He died that we may not die.
He was poor that we may be rich. God is not respecter of mankind.
Whoever comes to God in repentance shall be forgiven.
We need to reconcile with the Lord and accept Jesus Christ as Saviour and Lord. He loves us and he is waiting to receive us to His kingdom.
You need to reference the King of kings today. Receive Him into your life and you shall be saved.
Amen.
May the Lord bless you in Jesus name!

August 13

Good morning Father, Good morning Jesus, Good morning Holy Spirit.

Reading passage
Psalms 63:2-3

Find your watch Word
Psalms 62:8 (Memorise)

Prayer
The Lord is worthy to be trusted. Thy loving kindness is better than life.
We should allow our heart to be satisfied in Him.
God is above all and all our praise should go to Him on daily basis.
Magnify the Lord always because there is nothing difficult for Him.
By ourselves we can do nothing. Jesus is Lord.
Amen.
May the Lord bless you in Jesus name!

August 14

Good morning Father, Good morning Jesus, Good Morning Holy Spirit.

Reading passage
Psalms 45:6-7

Find your watch Word
Psalms 51:10 (Memorise)

Prayer
The Lord is righteous in all His ways.
Righteousness exalts a nation but sin is a reproach.
God is always bitter about the wicked on daily basis. The Scripture says "the wickedness of the wicked shall kill him.
The reading passage says Jesus loved righteousness and hated wickedness, so God anointed Him.
Pray that the Lord will exalt you in righteousness. The Scripture also says without holiness no one shall see the Lord. Amen.
May the Lord bless you in Jesus name!

August 15

Good morning Father, Good morning Jesus, Good morning Holy Spirit.

Reading passage
Mark 4:11-12

Find your watch Word
John 8:29b (Memorise)

Prayer
Jesus Christ died for us on the cross of Calvary. If we give our lives to Him and do that which pleases Him, He will give us whatever we ask from Him. God promised us everything in His Kingdom, but requires our obedience.
My prayer is that we do not miss out on His good plans for our lives.
The knowledge, wisdom and understanding of God's Word in important.
These will enable us to reach and attain our potentials both spiritually and physically. Amen.
May the Lord bless you in Jesus name!

August 16

Good morning Father, Good morning Jesus, Good morning Holt Spirit.

Reading passage
Psalms 120:5-8

Find your watch Word
Psalms 130:5 (Memorise)

Prayer
*Jesus Christ is the giver and supplier of all good things. He is our source. We should always hope and wait on the Lord in every situation. Jesus will return to us to have mercy on us. With Him there is mercy and plenteous redemption.
Wait for Him today and He will redeem us from all evil. Amen.
May the Lord bless you in Jesus name!*

August 17

Good morning Father, Good morning Jesus, Good morning Holy Spirit.

Reading passage
Matthew 15:21-28

Find your watch Word
Matthew 15:26 (Memorise)

Prayer
Jesus met with this unbeliever who knows her stand and has wisdom to go about her faith and she was able to receive the favour of Jesus. Jesus actually told the woman that the grace is not meant for the dogs, but she accepted that the dog can benefit from the children's table. Child of God do you know your right in Christ? Pray for special grace meant for the children to come on you today. Amen.
May the Lord bless you in Jesus name!

August 18

Good morning Father, Good morning Jesus, Good morning Holy Spirit.

Reading passage
Deuteronomy 29:25-29

Find your watch Word
Deuteronomy 29:29 (Memorise)

Prayer
The revelation of God makes more knowledge available to us.
We must make sure we continue to walk with the Lord that the revelation of the secret of God be made available to us.
We need the move from information to mysteries of the Lord. God only reveals to those who are close to Him.
The revelation graduates us to apply His knowledge.
Pray today for the grace, serve the Lord in words of His covenant. Amen.
May the Lord bless you in Jesus name!

August 19

Good morning Father, Good morning Jesus, Good morning Holy Spirit.

Reading passage
Isaiah 48:11-18

Find your watch Word
John 17:21 (Memorise)

Prayer
The Lord said He has called us will do His pleasure to prosper us.
Take note of verse 13 of the reading passage. He said (God) His hand hath laid the foundation of the earth and when he calls onto them, the stand up together to answer Him.
What can God not do?
Verse 1 5 of the reading passage said "I' He is giving us assurance that nothing can change it. Be assured he will perfect that which concerns you. The Find your watch Word is also telling us to be one with God not looking for an alternative. Focus on prayers and believe God for good. Amen. May the Lord bless you in Jesus name!

August 20

Good morning Father, Good morning Jesus, Good morning Holy Spirit.

Reading passage
Habakkuk 2:1-4

Find your watch Word
Habakkuk 2:3 (Memorise)

Prayer
*The revelation and vision God has for us will always come at the appointed time.
Do we try as much as possible to stand upon our watch and see what the Lord will say to us?
It will always come to pass when He speaks.
The Scripture says it will be good for us to put our mind to all that we hear so that it will not be taken away from us any time.
The just shall live only by their faith, but if we depart from faith, God is not pleased with it.
Amen.
May the Lord bless you in Jesus name!*

August 21

Good morning Father, Good morning Jesus, Good morning Holy Spirit.

Reading passage
1 Corinthians 4:9-13

Find your watch Word
Psalms 119:99 (Memorise)

Prayer
Though the world might be looking at us as someone being cast out, but we are not. The Scripture says that we are knowledgeable than our teachers, Psalms 119:99.

God is sufficient for us. We are "fools" for Christ's sake, but He is our hope.

The Scripture says "eyes have not seen and ears have not heard and it has not gone into the hearts of men what God has prepared for those that are His".

Our prayer is that God should arise and show forth His glory in the world so that the world would be able to perceive that we are serving a good God. Amen.

May the Lord bless you in Jesus name!

August 22

Good morning Father, Good morning Jesus, Good morning Holy Spirit.

Reading passage
Genesis 17:15-19

Find your watch Word
Luke 1:37 (Memorise)

Prayer
Do you doubt what the Lord can do? Abraham and his wife did not. The 'Find your watch Word' of today is the Word of God that cannot be broken. With God nothing is impossible.
You may doubt what He said to you, but I want to assure you that what He said whether you believe it or not, shall come to pass.
It may come to a time in the life of a man after you have waited for a while and it looks as if what God has promised is not going to happen, then God comes suddenly to bring about a fulfilment.
Do not be discouraged, God is at work.
He will perfect that which concerns you. Amen.
Call upon Him today. Amen.
May the Lord bless you in Jesus name!

August 23

Good morning Father, Good morning Jesus, Good morning Holy Spirit.

Reading passage
Genesis 32:22-28

Find your watch Word
Acts 13:9 (Memorise)

Prayer
You need a change of name. Jacob's name was changed when he met with the Lord on his journey.
If you meet with the Lord, then something must be changed in your life. Jacob's name in the reading passage was changed; Saul's name was also changed to Paul.
For you to have a change of name, you need to be close to God, and His Word must live in you. The Ten Commandments of God are His command for you.
As you carry them out on daily basis, God is ready to walk with you and His hand will lead you on to your name change.
Pray for grace to live in Him. His grace enables you to change your circumstances.

August 24

Good morning Father, Good morning Jesus, Good morning, Holy Spirit.

Reading passage
1 John 3:1-5

Find your watch Word
Proverbs 13:21 (Memorise)

Prayer
We must make sure that we are pure in all things and manner.
God commanded us to be pure and the Scripture says without holiness no one shall see the Lord.
God is in the process of holiness all day and night. The Word of God is available to make us clean, washing us on daily basis.
We must live in the Word to guarantee our purity because nothing can make pure but the Word.
We have to keep asking for the grace to live in the Word every day. Amen.
May the Lord bless you in Jesus name!

August 25

Good morning Father, Good morning Jesus, Good morning Holy Spirit.

Reading passage
Matthew 11: 27-30

Find your watch Word
Philippians 4:19 (Memorise)

Prayer
The Lord is the only supplier and He will supply your needs according to His riches in glory by Christ Jesus, Philippians 4:19.
He said our own burden is heavy but His own is light. The world puts yokes on men, but God is the remover of yokes.
He stands in situations for us helping us to come out of devilish situations.
Jesus died on the cross of Calvary and shed His blood to pay for your freedom. Amen.
May the Lord bless you in Jesus name!

August 26

Good morning Father, Good morning Jesus, Good morning Holy Spirit.

Reading passage
2 Timothy 4:1-5

Find your watch Word
2 Timothy 3:14 (Memorise)

Prayer
The Scripture is alerting us to be watchful and hold fast to what we've learnt and where we learnt them.
God is faithful, for a time is coming when we will be judged of what we have been doing and how we live our lives.
We should be watchful and not careless. For the book of Revelation says that His coming is going to be sudden but if it does how would we know? Let us be vigilant and allow not the things of the flesh to carry us away.
Let us constantly search ourselves to be sure we are still in faith.
Pray for the grace today. Amen.
May the Lord bless you in Jesus name!

August 27

Good morning Father, Good morning Jesus, Good morning Holy Spirit.

Reading passage
1 Corinthians 2:5-14

Find your watch Word
1 Corinthians 2:5,6,10,14 (Memorise)

Prayer
We should not allow Satan to get grief for us, we should make sure we forgive. If we forgive, we will definitely be forgiven.
Let us try as much as possible to forgive others so that our prayers will be answered.
God has a standard of spirituality and weighs attitude, thought and behaviour and whatsoever you sow, that you shall reap.
We should put honesty and transparency in what we do.
We need to pray for grace to be spiritually straight forward and transparent. Amen.
May the Lord bless you in Jesus name!

August 28

Good morning Father, Good morning Jesus, Good morning Holy Spirit.

Reading passage
Romans 1:8-11, 16-18

Find your watch Word
Romans 1:16-18 (Memorise)

Prayer
Faith is the only thing that moves the Lord in us. Without faith, it is impossible to please God. Those that have faith will be able to get their need met by God always. Without faith you cannot reach God.
Faith is an instrument that connects us to God. Paul in Romans 1:8 was thanking God for the faith of the Romans which was spoken off throughout the world.
If there is no faith through Jesus Christ, there is no Christianity.
We are empty without faith. I pray your faith will not fail. Pray today for the faith that never fails.
Amen.
May the Lord bless you in Jesus name!

August 29

Good morning, Good morning Jesus, Good morning Holy Spirit.

Reading passage
2 Chronicles 20:12-17

Find your watch Word
2 Chronicles 20:15 (Memorise)

Prayer
The Lord has a way of fighting our battles. The only thing we need is to trust in Him for the instruction He will give us.
When God gives instruction, He has already sent out forces to carry out the operation. God has a way.
He used only one Angel to fight with Sennacherib and all the Syrian army.
The Lord destroyed the whole of Syrian army by an angel (2 Kings 19:35).
The Scripture records that the whole army were all dead bodies by the morning. God is the God of justice. Stand with God and you will never regret it.
Pray for the grace to stand and wait patiently for God. Amen.
May the Lord bless you in Jesus name!

August 30

Good morning Father, Good morning Jesus, Good morning Holy Spirit.

Reading passage
Isaiah 28:18

Find your watch Word
Hosea 13:14 (Memorise)

Prayer
The Lord has promised that we shall live and not die. Death shall not have dominion over us, it is essential to know the impact of the shed Blood of Jesus upon us.

In the book of Isaiah 28:18, the Lord said our covenant with death shall be disannulled and if you consider the Find your watch Word, Hosea 13:14, God has ransomed us from the power of the grave.

Death has no power over us. God has come to give us life not death. We are victorious, so let's continue to celebrate our freedom in Christ Jesus. Do not be afraid, put on the whole armour of faith, confidence, salvation etc. Start to declare life over yourself. Amen.

May the Lord bless you in Jesus name!

August 31

Good morning Father, Good morning Jesus, Good morning Holy Spirit.

Reading passage
1 John 4:7-8

Find your watch Word
1 John 4:8 (Memorise)

Prayer
God is love. The scripture specifies the type of people who know God or do not know God. If love is absent in a family or an organisation, every type of evil will be present there. If there is no love, prayers cannot be answered. God is love, so whosoever does not love cannot claim to be praying to God who is love. You can't be a child of God and be happy to keep malice, speaking all sorts of dirty words and still bully or hate somebody. Ask God to search and purge you. He is faithful. He will always answer your cry. Pray that the agape love of God and for the grace to live a life of love. Amen. May the Lord bless you in Jesus name!

September 1

Good morning Father, Good morning Jesus, Good morning Holy Spirit.

Reading passage
Luke 21:12-15

Find your watch Word
Luke 21:13 (Memorise)

Prayer
Whatever you are passing through now is for a short time, it will all turn to testimony.
God does not try anyone with evil.
Evil takes its source from the devil and victory from the Lord.
But God said it will turn to testimony. He does not lie and does not fail.
He will bring it to pass for you. Hold to this promise and remind God.
Keep putting action and pray along until God finishes His work. Amen.
May the Lord bless you in Jesus name!

September 2

Good morning Father, Good morning Jesus, Good morning Holy Spirit.

Reading passage
Luke 21: 33-36

Find your watch Word
Luke 21:36a (Memorise)

Prayer
The Bible enjoins us to pray always. In the book of 1Thessalonian 5:17 the Bible says, "praying always". This is to guide against any sudden happenings.

The time will come suddenly. This scripture says, so that it does not catch us unaware.

We must be counted worthy and be able to stand at judgement throne.

Among the important points to consider is not to allow the worldly things to carry us away from the spirit.

We must be spiritually sensitive in whatever we are doing and remember our source. Pray for these important points and may the Lord grant you His grace. Amen.

May the Lord bless you in Jesus name!

September 3

Good morning Father, Good morning Jesus, Good morning Holy Spirit.

Reading passage
1 John 3:1-3

Find your watch Word
1 John 3:3 (Memorise)

Prayer
The Lord loves us so much that He gave His only begotten Son to us. This love must be continued and be given to others.
Without faith and love we cannot please the Lord. Anyone that hopes in the Lord must purify himself/herself as the Lord is pure.
Our hope in Christ ties us to Him by His love which made Him to lay down His life for us. Strife and hatred are contrary to love.
We need the grace to live the life of purity and love. God will enhance the spirit with the grace as you go in your prayer today. Amen.
May the Lord bless you in Jesus name!

September 4

Good morning Father, Good morning Jesus, Good morning Holy Spirit.

Reading passage
Isaiah 25:1-9

Find your watch Word
Isaiah 25:8 (Memorise)

Prayer
The Lord is faithful in all His ways. Consider verse 8 of this reading passage, whatever our problem is, the scripture says He will wipe tears away from off all faces and the rebuke of His people.
He will save us and we will be glad.
Verse 9 of the reading passage and Luke 1:37 says that nothing shall be impossible with God. Today, all tears shall be wiped off your face and be replaced with joy in Jesus name. Amen.
May the Lord bless you in Jesus name!

September 5

Good morning Father, Good morning Jesus, Good morning Holy Spirit.

Reading passage
Malachi 1:11-14

Find your watch Word
Malachi 1:14b (Memorise)

Prayer
The scripture tries to magnify the Lord and His name.
Verse 11 tells us how great the name of God is among the Gentiles and the Heathen. In verse14b, the Lord said that "I am a great King" and He said His name is dreadful among the heathen, in the midst of demons.
So when you praise God this morning, praise Him as the King and when you pray, let your faith and confidence tell you that your prayer is answered. No king as God.
The scripture says His name is "dreadful" among the heathen. Praise God. Amen.
May the Lord bless you in Jesus name!

September 6

Good morning Father, Good morning Jesus, Good morning Holy Spirit.

Reading passage
Proverbs 3:9-10

Find your watch Word
Proverbs 3:9 (Memorise)

Prayer
We should honour the Lord with what we have.
I want you to ponder on those two verses this morning.
In the book of Malachi 3:11, the Bible says "And I will rebuke every devourer for your sakes and he shall not destroy the fruits before the time in the field saith the Lord of Host".
I pray you will not experience poverty to understand and appreciate the lesson of this morning.
Think very well before you go to pray this morning and may the Holy Spirit help you in your prayer today. Amen.
May the Lord bless you in Jesus name!

September 7

Good morning Father, Good morning Jesus, Good morning Holy Spirit.

Reading passage
1 Thessalonians 5:15-17

Find your watch Word
1 Thessalonians 5:15 (Memorise)

Prayer
Jesus has commanded us to be at peace with all men.
In the passage of this morning, Paul encouraged us to render no evil for evil. As a child of covenant, stand firm in the Lord and be of good effect. Righteousness the scripture says exalts a nation but sin is a reproach. God wants us to live a righteous life.
If anyone has ever offended us in any way, we as children of God should not repay evil for evil. If we do, this will work against us.
Be of good cheer God has overcome the world. Live a life that is above sin, and shun all unrighteous behaviour.
You are victorious. Amen.
May the Lord bless you in Jesus name!

September 8

Good morning Father, Good morning Jesus, Good morning Holy Spirit.

Reading passage
John 6:48-58

Find your watch Word
John 6:51 (Memorise)

Prayer

Here Jesus is laying emphasis on the taking of Communion. This is one of the wisdom of God. Many people are dying alive because of lack of knowledge.

Jesus saying in this portion of the scripture that He is the Bread of life who came down from heaven, "I am the Bread of life".

Again consider the second half of verse 50 which says that "a man may eat thereof, and not die". I pray as you obey this command you will not die any death in Jesus name.

Call upon the name of God, declare your desire and take the Communion at any time to receive life in your body (fullness of life). Amen.

May the Lord bless you in Jesus name!

September 9

Good morning Father, Good morning Jesus, Good morning Holy Spirit.

Reading passage
Revelation 12:7-19

Find your watch Word
Revelation 12:11 (Memorise)

Prayer
Satan caused problem in heaven before God sent him down in to the world. The Lord took victory and gave it to us.
The Bible says that we overcame by the Blood of Jesus that won for us.
When you pray, use your mouth to speak the Word of God. Your victory will come through the confession and praying with the Blood of Jesus. The name of Jesus is great; the Blood of Jesus is the last card. Satan cannot withstand the Blood of Jesus. Amen.
May the Lord bless you in Jesus name!

September 10

Good morning Father, Good morning Jesus, Good morning Holy Spirit.

Reading passage
1 Corinthians 16:7-9

Find your watch Word
1 Corinthians 11:9 (Memorise)

Prayer
Most of the time the children of God pray, the prayer is answered.
The book of Daniel talks about how the Lord always heard Daniel's prayer each time he prayed but it was the prince of Persia that always delayed his result. God answers our prayers; He doesn't store prayers.
The door is opened to us all the time to possess our possession but we have to warfare against the adversaries that are standing on the way. God is only telling us this to enable us do what we suppose to do to have our victories.
Always remember the Lord is on your side. Make a firm decision and stand until your breakthrough comes. Amen.
May the Lord bless you in Jesus name!

September 11

Good morning Father, Good morning Jesus, Good morning Holy Spirit.

Reading passage
Isaiah 45:11-12

Find your watch Word
Isaiah 45:11 (Memorise)

Prayer
The Lord is giving us the assurance in our prayer requests. He wants us to ask in the name of Jesus. When we pray, we have to ask with confidence. We should not be afraid or allow doubt in our prayers. God said "Command me", we should be bold in God to declare our request in prayer. He is the Lord that made the heaven and the earth.

Verse 12b of that same Isaiah says it. There is nothing impossible for God to do. Luke 1:37 says it is impossible for God to lie.

Take Him by His Word and you will return to God with thanksgiving. Amen.

May the Lord bless you in Jesus name!

September 12

Good morning Father, Good morning Jesus, Good morning Holy Spirit.

Reading passage
Matthew 6:5-6

Find your watch Word
Matthew 6:6a (Memorise)

Prayer
It is important to know the rudiment of how prayers can be answered.
God has a standard and the standard must be understood by the saints before our prayers can be answered.
God does not want us to be hypocrites.
He wants us to be meek in all we do because this is the way of the Lord.
Pride is a reproach to God; He does not answer the prayers of a proud person. So read this passage properly for you to move God.
Use this standard to pray always and God will teach you and you will return to God with thanksgiving. Amen.
May the Lord bless you in Jesus name!

September 13

Good morning Father, Good morning Jesus, Good morning Holy Spirit.

Reading passage
Isaiah 14:24-27

Find your watch Word
Isaiah 14:27 (Memorise)

Prayer
When the Lord swears it is dangerous for man to try to withstand Him. The Assyrians in our lives are in trouble.
The Assyrians were the adversaries in the life of the Israelites.
God determined and purposed to destroy them and He did and set His people free.
Verse 27 says the Lord has purposed, who shall disannul, He has stretched his hand out, who shall turn it back? He (God) has set to deliver you and set you at liberty.
Do you believe Him? Just hold fast your faith and wait for His glory. It will show up.
Give thanks this morning for what God has done already. Hallelujah! Amen.
May the Lord bless you in Jesus name!

September 14

Good morning Father, Good morning Jesus, Good morning Holy Spirit.

Reading passage
Exodus 4:21-23

Find your watch Word
Exodus 4:23 (Memorise)

Prayer
You are the first born of the Lord because you are the heir of David and Jesus.
So no one can mess you up. You need to know who you are in the Lord.
When you identify your identity like this in the Word, you pray and claim your right in the Lord. Focus and centre your request and prayer on Him when you pray this morning.
God who knows His covenant will arise and fight your battles and you will return to Him with thanks giving. Amen.
May the Lord bless you in Jesus name!

September 15

Good morning Father, Good morning Jesus, Good morning Holy Spirit.

Reading passage
Psalms 124:1-7

Find your watch Word
Psalms 124:7 (Memorise)

Prayer
God is on your side. He will not give you as a prey to the enemy and adversaries' teeth.
You have escaped. I say you are escaped from the snare of the fowler.
This is the word of God and revelation for this morning.
Close not your mouth today but begin to declare His Word which says "we are escaped".
Possess your possessions today.
It is well with you. Amen.
May the Lord bless you in Jesus name!

September 16

Good morning Father, Good morning Jesus, Good morning Holy Spirit.

Reading passage
Isaiah 40:28-31

Find your watch Word
Isaiah 40:29 (Memorise)

Prayer
The scripture says God gives strength to the faint. God Himself neither faint nor weary. God is able to make all grace abound towards you.
Keep your heart stable. God is God my brothers and sisters.
Keep your faith focussed, trust in the Lord, He will never fail you. Wait for Him.
The Bible says in 1 Chronicles 5:520b, God does not fail. They cried unto Him and trusted in Him. Do you trust that God can do it?
It might look as if it is getting late, you caused it because of your up and down type of faith. Speak to yourself even if God will not do it, I will not go back to Satan.
Remember the three Hebrew men. They said in the book of Daniel 3:17-18, wait on God; He's able. Amen.
May the Lord bless you in Jesus name!

September 17

Good morning Father, Good morning Jesus, Good morning Holy Spirit.

Reading passage
John 17:14-16

Find your watch Word
John 17:16 (Memorise)

Prayer
You are not of the world. Jesus Christ said it in the scripture. You need to know who you are. When the children of this world come to you, display your wisdom and flee from them.
The scripture says children of this world are wise, they know what they are doing.
The book of James says there are different types of wisdom. They will want to use their own worldly wisdom to take you away from Jesus.
You need to use the wisdom of God to flee and say no to them.
Pray that you will not fall into temptation. Amen.
May the Lord bless you in Jesus name!

September 18

Good morning Father, Good morning Jesus, Good morning Holy Spirit.

Reading passage
Jeremiah 10:21-24

Find your watch Word
Jeremiah 10:23-24 (Memorise)

Prayer
Your way is not in your hand to choose or take decision. All your ways are in the hands of the Lord. You need to recognise and identify God as your source of everything.
Ponder or think properly on verses 23 & 24 of Jeremiah 10. In Jeremiah 10:24, he said correct me, in judgement not in anger.
If you take your own way, it might at a time get to a place whereby God will be angry.
I pray you will not experience the anger of God. Leave all to Him that is perfect to perfect your ways.
Pray for the Spirit of meekness and humility. Ask God to give you the grace for wisdom to seek Him only.
Yield yourself to Him to direct and lead you. It is well with you. Amen.
May the Lord bless you in Jesus name!

September 19

Good morning Father, Good morning Jesus, Good morning Holy Spirit.

Reading passage
1 Corinthians 9:22-25

Find your watch Word
1 Corinthians 9:24-25 (Memorise)

Prayer
The Lord wants you to discipline yourself in all things. Self discipline is the key to the top in life. Read the passage for reading this morning. No careless man will get to the top. God knows those that can work with Him.
He told Gideon these people are too many, go and reduce them. Amen.
May the Lord bless you in Jesus name!

September 20

Good morning Father, Good morning Jesus, Good morning Holy Spirit.

Reading passage
Ephesians 1:8-14

Find your watch Word
Ephesians 1:13-14 (Memorise)

Prayer
God has made available for us the mystery of His will. It's left for us to take it as our inheritance. All we need to do is to trust in the Lord's word of truth and walk in it.
This is our inheritance because the word of God takes us to our purpose in God.
There is our place of manifestation.
Pray for the grace to understand the power of His word, to get to your place of shinning in the Lord.
The Lord will grant you understanding in Jesus name. Amen.
May the Lord bless you in Jesus name!

September 21

Good morning Father, Good morning Jesus, Good morning Holy Spirit.

Reading passage
John 17:13-17

Find your watch Word
John 17:16 (Memorise)

Prayer
You are not of the world, so keep yourself away from the world. Jesus Christ has prayed for you. Read the whole chapter of John 17.
God wants you to keep your heart on the things of the Spirit.
Be confident in yourself and put your trust in the Lord.
Pray the prayer that Jesus Christ prays for you here, "Do not fear".
Put on the whole armour of His might. Amen.
May the Lord bless you in Jesus name!

September 22

Good morning Father, Good morning, Good morning Holy Spirit.

Reading passage
Exodus 7:1-7

Find your watch Word
Exodus 7:1 (Memorise)

Prayer
The Lord has made you "god" in every life's situations and over all your enemies.
Do not allow anxiety, fear or doubt to hold you ransom.
Always put yourself in your positions of a "god".
If God says you are 'gods', He meant you to dominate all sorts of life situation.
There's none like the Lord. Hope and trust in Him and take your position.
You will be out of Egypt and possess your Canaan land. It is well with you.
Pray and receive grace of dominion. Amen.
May the Lord bless you in Jesus name!

September 23

Good morning Father, Good morning Jesus, Good morning Holy Spirit.

Reading passage
Revelation 12:7-9

Find your watch Word
Revelation 12:7-9 (Memorise)

Prayer
The war in heaven was because of you. The victory was given to Jesus.
This is because Satan wanted the dominion of the world to be in his hand, to take authority. God has authority over the earth but He created us for His glory alone.
He has fought a lot of battles because of us. Satan cannot have us.
Look unto Jesus the author and finisher of our faith. Confess this Word. "Satan you cannot have me". Jesus Christ has overcome for me."
You fought with Jesus, you failed, how will you fight with me and win? You are a liar. I have overcome by the Blood of Jesus.
Pray after this confession.
You have overcome by the Blood of Jesus and by the words of our testimony. Amen.
May the Lord bless you in Jesus name!

September 24

Good morning Father, Good morning Jesus, Good morning Holy Spirit.

Reading passage
Isaiah 65:19-25

Find your watch Word
Isaiah 65:19b (Memorise)

Prayer
There shall be no crying in my home; it shall be joy all through.
Make confession to yourself and turn it to prayer this morning. Verse 12 says 'they shall build houses and inhabit them', that is to you. Claim it for yourself.
You shall live long to enjoy the work of your hands. This particular part of the Bible is for your inheritance in the Lord.
Call upon the name of the Lord today. It is well with you physically and spiritually.
Death is not yours. It is life that Jesus gave to you. Relax in God. Amen.
May the Lord bless you in Jesus name!

September 25

Good morning Father, Good morning Jesus, Good morning Holy Spirit.

Reading passage
Daniel 10:1-5

Find your watch Word
Daniel 10:1-3 (Memorise)

Prayer
Daniel ate no bread. What does this mean? He was fasting because of his situation and the Lord appeared to him.
Have you ever fasted because of what you were asking God? You need to do away with food for a while.
It might be your breakfast, lunch or dinner so that you can receive divine direction from the Lord, pray for strength.
For some people it is difficult.
Miss your breakfast, or lunch or supper to meet with God on issues of your life. Amen.
May the Lord bless you in Jesus name!

September 26

Good morning Father, Good morning Jesus, Good morning Holy Spirit.

Reading passage
Exodus 3:6-9

Find your watch Word
Exodus 3:8a (Memorise)

Prayer
The Lord purposed to deliver the Israelites after they had called upon Him.
If you read today's reading passage, you will realise that our cry has to go up to the Lord before He will come down.
The God of vengeance will visit you this season in the name of Jesus.
Psalms 94 says you need to connect to heaven this morning for the God of vengeance to come down for your deliverance.
Make sure He hears your cry.

September 27

Good morning Father, Good morning Jesus, Good morning Holy Spirit.

Reading passage
Exodus 19:3-7

Find your watch Word
Exodus 19:5 (Memorise)

Prayer
*The Lord is ready to brag about you to the kingdom of Satan.
He gave us just an instruction which is highlighted in verse 5 of today's reading passage.
We should always pursue the love of God which is to obey His command.
God does not change, it is man that changes.
When He promises He brings it to pass.
Ask God for the grace to always obey Him. Amen.
May the Lord bless you in Jesus name!*

September 28

Good morning Father, Good morning Jesus, Good morning Holy Spirit.

Reading passage
2 Peter 1:3-8

Find your watch Word
2 Peter 1:4 (Memorise)

Prayer
The Lord has given us the opportunity through His divine power to escape a lot of worldly lust and corruption.
We are made to be edified by His knowledge which makes us to grow in the kingdom. We are able to put together all the fruits of love. These help us to grow in the Lord unto perfection of all in the Spirit of God.
Temperance, patience, brotherly kindness, faith, virtue and godliness.
A child of God cannot be barren in all his doings if he allows this to function or work in our lives. Pray the fruit of the Spirit into your life today.
Amen.
May the Lord bless you in Jesus name!

September 29

Good morning Father, Good morning Jesus, Good morning Holy Spirit.

Reading passage
Psalms 34:10-11

Find your watch Word
Psalms 34:10 (Memorise)

Prayer
The Lord promised you will not lack. He does not fail in His promises. The plan of God for your life will stand. Are you in lack of anything now? Do not worry. He is our "supplier", the creator of heaven and earth.
The scripture says, do you not know that the Lord of heaven and earth never slumbers nor sleeps. Greater is He that is in us than the one in the world.
Put your request before God today, be happy and do not fear.
He will supply all your needs according to His riches in glory by Christ Jesus (Philippians 4:19). Amen.
May the Lord bless you in Jesus name!

September 30

Good morning Father, Good morning Jesus, Good morning Holy Spirit.

Reading passage
1 Thessalonians 1:6-9

Find your watch Word
1 Thessalonians 1:6 (Memorise)

Prayer
The scripture says it's a good thing for God to repay our enemies with destruction.
Your adversaries shall not go unpunished.
Keep your heart at peace and always rejoice in the Lord for He is able to deliver you.
He will not shed His blood for nothing.
God has promised.
Go to pray, call upon His name. Amen.
May the Lord bless you in Jesus name!

October 1

Good morning, Good morning Jesus, Good morning Holy Spirit.

Reading passage
1 Thessalonians 5:16-18; Revelations 3:16-17

Find your watch Word
1 Thessalonians 5:16-17 (Memorise)

Prayer
Prayer is the key to every good thing in life. The scriptures recorded that Jesus started with prayer today for quiet places to pray to be able to hear God lead Him throughout His ministry. Revelations 3:16-17 said if you are lukewarm, God will spit you out of His mouth.
Children, start building your prayer life. God will help you. Amen.
May the Lord bless you in Jesus name!

October 2

Good morning, Good morning Jesus, Good morning Holy Spirit.

Reading passage
1 Peter 2:21-25

Find your watch Word
1 Peter 2:24b (Memorise)

Prayer
Jesus Christ gave Himself on the cross of Calvary that we might live.
The scripture says "by His stripes we are healed". If Jesus Christ died for us on the cross, it wouldn't have been for fun or play. He could have used the bull or sheep if it was for fun.
For example, there were many whose hope was lost, but because of Christ they became testimonies to the greatness of the name of our God. If we die with Him, we will reign with Him. The journey of faith must be taken with all seriousness.
If truly we are born again we should be alive to the Word of Christ the Redeemer. Lift up your face and look on to the Lord today. Cry to Him and reference His Word and promises in every area of your life. Amen.
May the Lord bless you in Jesus name!

October 3

Good morning Father, Good morning Jesus, Good morning Holy Spirit.

Reading passage
Psalms 16: 7-9

Find your watch Word
Psalms 16:8 (Memorise)

Prayer
Keep the Lord before you. Psalms 16:8 says, I have set the Lord always before me. In other words, focus on Him.
You must focus on the Lord always and keep Him on the right hand. In my country there is an adage that says whatever is put on the right hand side cannot be lost.
So keep your God on your right hand and you can never be moved. If your God is unique, He cannot be put on the left hand. If you magnify God, He will magnify you.
Tell Him how much you love Him. Amen.
May the Lord bless you in Jesus name!

October 4

Good morning Father, Good morning Jesus, Good morning Holy Spirit.

Reading passage
Isaiah 40:28-31

Find your watch Word
Isaiah 40:29 (Memorise)

Prayer
The Lord is the creator of heaven and the earth. He is the only one that gives power to the faint. If you do not know, it is only with God that you can finish your course in life. Make God your first in life. Psalms 16:8.

He will not disappointment but will release your from captivity and announce you to your world. In all situations learn to wait on God, He will take you through. The youth can faint but God will renew your strength.

He is the only hope of the world. It looks as if it's not to people. Try and see the Lord is good. Pray a prayer of faith today in His presence and see what God is set to do in your life. Amen.

May the Lord bless you in Jesus name!

October 5

Good morning Father, Good morning Jesus, Good morning Holy Spirit.

Reading passage
Isaiah 46: 7-11

Find your watch Word
Isaiah 46:10 (Memorise)

Prayer
The Lord makes the war to cease. Is there any problem you are facing at this particular time, God makes war to cease.
He is with you. All you need to do is trust God and wait for what He wants to do in your life.
Tarry at the prayer altar; wait on God to receive direction from Him.
Consistently feed yourself in the Word. Amen.
May the Lord bless you in Jesus name!

October 6

Good morning Father, Good morning Jesus, Good morning Holy Spirit.

Reading passage
Jeremiah 1:5-10

Find your watch Word
Jeremiah 1:10 (Memorise)

Prayer

Verse 5 of the book of Jeremiah 1 which is the study for this morning says God knew us before we were formed in our mother's womb.
The scripture says "He that made the eyes will He not see".
Every thing about us is known to God. He wants us to pray before He answers. In verse 10, God has given us authority over nations and kingdoms, to pull down and root out the works of darkness.
We are in charge. Satan has no right except we allow him by what we say and do. All we need is confidence to do the right thing and it will get to our hands.
Lift up your voice and pray.

October 7

Good morning Father, Good morning Jesus, Good morning Holy Spirit.

Reading passage
Romans 8:14-16

Find your watch Word
Romans 8:15 (Memorise)

Prayer
We are joint heirs with Christ. We are children of God, we are not slaves.
So we have access to Christ, we should not allow the spirit of fear to plague us. Fear itself is bondage. Jesus Christ wants us to come to Him and ask whatsoever we want Him to do for us.
If we are not confident in ourselves to speak to Him, we cannot receive. Fear torments, we should be able to pray confidently. If we cannot pray, we will not have faith in ourselves.
A prayerful Christian is a powerful Christian and a confident Christian.
Without consistent prayer, we will be void of peace. No peace, no security from the power of the devil. There is then the possibility of fear on every side. Pray for boldness, confidence and victory over fear. Amen.
May the Lord bless you in Jesus name!

October 8

Good morning Father, Good morning Jesus, Good morning Holy Spirit.

Reading passage
Matthew 6:6-9

Find your watch Word
Matthew 6:7 (Memorise)

Prayer
The Lord commanded us to pray but not with vain repetition. Our faith is very important on the prayer altar.

If we are strong in our faith in God, we do not need any vain repetition.

God knows what our concerns are, but He just wants us to speak with our mouth what we want so that it will not be the matter of laziness on our side.

We work before we are paid. So we have to also get involved by praying before we can have our prayers answered. Amen.

May the Lord bless you in Jesus name!

October 9

Good morning Father, Good morning Jesus, Good morning Holy Spirit.

Reading passage
Philippians 4:4-7

Find your watch Word
Philippians 4:6 (Memorise)

Prayer
The scripture says we should be careful for nothing. In other words, you should not worry about anything, if and when you have committed such a thing to God in prayer. Do not compare your life with any other person. Be yourself in all you do, God is in control of the situation of your life. It is not your worrying that will change things. That your friend bought a car for instance should not make you want to do the same. Do all things in moderation. Pray for the grace to be yourself today. Let God be your focus all the time. It is well with you. The scripture says the peace of God will keep your heart from worry, Amen.

October 10

Good morning Father, Good morning Jesus, Good morning Holy Spirit.

Reading passage
Romans 8:13-17

Find your watch Word
Romans 8:15 (Memorise)

Prayer
Why are you fearful? It was always said in the scripture that fear torments.
Fear is a punishment for those who cannot exercise their faith. "Keep your heart wit all diligence for out it are the issues of life". Fear is deadly because the Bible says the devil comes to steal, to kill and to destroy.
The devil himself is the author of fear, so why put your life in danger.
Jesus Christ has come to give peace and life in abundance. For example, when you experience anything that can make you fear, just say: come what may, God is with me.
The three Hebrew boys said even if God will not deliver them, they would never bow to the golden image made by the King – Daniel 3:17-18. Make up your mind who to fear, God or the devil.
Pray that the eye of your understanding to be enlightened. Amen.
May the Lord bless you in Jesus name!

October 11

Good morning Father, Good morning Jesus, Good morning Holy Spirit.

Reading passage
Isaiah 65:20-24

Find your watch Word
Isaiah 65:24 (Memorise)

Prayer
The promises of God are yes and Amen! The Lord's promise to us in verse 4 of this morning's reading is that we shall call on Him and He shall answer.

Remember you are a child of promise; all you need to do is to hold fast to the promises of God and believe that He that promised is able to bring it to pass. God is not a man that will promise and fail you. He is the God who fulfils His promise.

I have experienced His goodness all of my life through His very good promises.

God is a Spirit and those who serve Him must do so in spirit and in truth – (John 4:24). Take time to meditate on this morning's study passage, then place before the Lord two things you can trust Him for.

Check your life if you have sin in any way, ask Him for forgiveness and hope for your request and see what God will do for you. Amen.

May the Lord bless you in Jesus name!

October 12

Good morning Father, Good morning Jesus, Good morning Holy Spirit.

Reading passage
1 Corinthians 15:56-58

Find your watch Word
1 Corinthians 15:56 (Memorise)

Prayer

What is your knowledge about sin? The scripture says 'The sting of death is sin ...' – (1 Corinthians 15:56). Indeed, as a Christian you should not play with sin in your life. The Word of God is perfect and God is truth. He does not say or speak a word that will fall to the ground. If you are really a child of God, face God and serve Him. There is nothing too difficult for Him. He has never disappointed any of His children except for those who are not really known to Him.

There are some children of God that are not known in the kingdom because of some sinful habits; such people are denied His power in their life. They are not covered by His Blood because the wages of sin is always death. Think about it today "The sting of death is sin". Go to God and speak to Him today after you've checked your life. Amen.

May the Lord bless you in Jesus name!

October 13

Good morning Father, Good morning Jesus, Good morning Holy Spirit.

Reading passage
1 Corinthians 3:10-17

Find your watch Word
1 Corinthians 3:16 (Memorise)

Prayer
The Lord is pure in all His ways. He has made man His temple in which nothing like sin should have a place. We are His temple where He resides. Mind what you build on Jesus who is your foundation.

Sin is a reproach unto any person. If you have truly known the Lord, then mind how you live your life because your lifestyle is what you are building upon Jesus whom you accepted into your live.

Think on what you have built in the past or what you are building at the moment. You cannot deceive God but you can only deceive yourself. Return to God today. He's merciful to receive you back to Himself. Amen.

May the Lord bless you in Jesus name!

October 14

Good morning Father, Good morning Jesus, Good morning Holy Spirit.

Reading passage
Psalms 35:1-10

Find your watch Word
Psalms 35:4 (Memorise)

Prayer
God is ready to fight your contenders who are your enemies. They will be confounded and the Angel of God will chase them and trouble them. No mountain is higher than God.
It's never in history that something is difficult for God. Take God by His Word; He has never lost a battle. God cannot disappoint you.
Hold to the Word in this passage and you will return to Him with thanksgiving. Amen.
May the Lord bless you in Jesus name!

October 15

Good morning Father, Good morning Jesus, Good morning Holy Spirit.

Reading passage
Psalms 77:12-14

Find your watch Word
Psalms 77:12 (Memorise)

Prayer
The Word of God is the power and wisdom of God. Except a man reads, meditate and digest it, man cannot make progress and a change in life. Meditation on the Word of God makes a way for man.

He has the power in heaven and on earth. God is His Word and it is His Word that makes the life of God. God displays His power in the life of man. We should be ready to work out a change in our life through the Word of God.

Psalms 105:8 says "God will always be mindful of His covenant. He watches over His word to perform it". Amen.

May the Lord bless you in Jesus name!

October 16

Good morning Father, Good morning Jesus, Good morning Holy Spirit.

Reading passage
Job 22:27-30

Find your watch Word
Job 22:27 (Memorise)

Prayer
There is an assurance of the answer to your prayers. God is a God that answers prayers. If you pray, your prayers will definitely be answered. Believe in your prayers and let the Lord answer your prayers.
Try God today and you will be amazed about it. Our God is a faithful God. All we need to do is to trust Him with all our heart.
Jesus has sacrificed for us. So read your Bible, meditate on it and pray, and see God's blessings flow into your life. Amen.
May the Lord bless you in Jesus name!

October 17

Good morning Father, Good morning Jesus, Good morning Holy Spirit.

Reading passage
Proverbs 20:19-20

Find your watch Word
Proverbs 20:19 (Memorise)

Prayer
*A child of God must not be among those that talk too much. You should not be the one who backbite other people. Take time to occupy yourself with things of the kingdom instead of talking too much. Meditate on the Word of God.
This will help you to live a life free from sin because you carry the image of God.
Be careful and ask the Holy Spirit to help you keep the door of your mouth shut.
Think before you speak and let your words be always seasoned. Amen.
May the Lord bless you in Jesus name!*

October 18

Good morning Father, Good morning Jesus, Good morning Holy Spirit.

Reading passage
2 Timothy 2:19-21

Find your watch Word
2 Timothy 2:21 (Memorise)

Prayer
Evil desires are compounded at the youthful stage of life. We should. Therefore, learn as much as possible to identify and discern evil behaviour and desires and run away from them all.

2 Timothy 2:21 says we should flee every evil desire. Verse 19 says everyone that is named by the name of God should depart from iniquity. God really warns us from evil and everything attached to evil.

God will give us understanding. As children we have to choose to live the life of Christ. Yes, we want to do good things, but good and evil are opposed to each other.

Evil has a way of overriding our desire to do good things. Call the Spirit of God to teach you to pray against this today. Amen.

May the Lord bless you in Jesus name!

October 19

Good morning Father, Good morning Jesus, Good morning Holy Spirit.

Reading passage
James 3:14-16

Find your watch Word
James 3:16 (Memorise)

Prayer
The Word of God is able to discern between the wisdom from heaven and the earthly. Heavenly wisdom is pure while the earthly is not.
We should yield ourselves to the hand of the Holy Spirit for guidance to identify the right wisdom per time.
Pray against the earthly wisdom and let the Lord help you to discern the two. Amen.
May the Lord bless you in Jesus name!

October 20

Good morning Father, Good morning Jesus, Good morning Holy Spirit.

Reading passage
2 Chronicles 20:20-22

Find your watch Word
2 Chronicles 20:22 (Memorise)

Prayer
The Lord is mighty and able to do all things – Luke 1:37. Make the Lord your first priority in life. It is recorded in our reading passage from 2 Chronicles that God sent an ambush against the enemies of the children of Israel.

He is our sufficiency. If He did it for the children of Israel, He will do it for you. Praise Him like never before.

Praise moves God to do anything for you. Arise afresh today and praise God as never before. Amen.

May the Lord bless you in Jesus name!

October 21

Good morning Father, Good morning Jesus, Good morning Holy Spirit.

Reading passage
Psalms 89:13-15

Find your watch Word
Psalms 89:15 (Memorise)

Prayer
Joy is the identity of God. When your joy is resounding, then He will identify with you. Children of God, it does not matter what your challenges are, just put on the garment of joy. God will arise to let you out of any prison the enemy may have put you in.
Pray for the grace to embrace the unspeakable joy of God. Amen.
May the Lord bless you in Jesus name!

October 22

Good morning Father, Good morning Jesus, Good morning Holy Spirit.

Reading passage
Psalms 89:17-18

Find your watch Word
Psalms 89:18 (Memorise)

Prayer
The Lord is our defence. Man cannot defend us how ever hard they try. God is the strength of our lives (Verse 17).
The power of darkness has nothing good to offer. It takes the grace of God to make way for us. Hebrew 2:14-15 says by His death, He frees those held captive and in slavery.
He has many ways to free us from destruction. Jesus is Lord. Amen.
May the Lord bless you in Jesus name!

October 23

Good morning Father, Good morning Jesus, Good morning Holy Spirit.

Reading passage
Ephesians 4:31-32

Find your watch Word
Ephesians 4:32 (Memorise)

Prayer
We must live a life of kindness to each other, forgiving one another. God cannot forgive us if we do not forgive others.
He has commanded us to be kind to one another, forgiving our brothers and sisters. If we refused to forgive, our prayer will not be heard.
God is very serious about all His commands. I pray He will give you the understanding.
Let go of all the offences you hold against your friends and people.
So that you will live a life of peace and that your prayers will be answered. Amen.
May the Lord bless you in Jesus name!

October 24

Good morning Father, Good morning Jesus, Good morning Holy Spirit.

Reading passage
Matthew 4:17-20

Find your watch Word
Matthew 4:19 (Memorise)

Prayer
God promised to make you fishers of men. This is the truth, if you can just make up your mind and allow the Lord Himself to speak through you and thereby spread the Gospel of Jesus Christ to others. Jesus Christ has made it easy for us. He will give you what to say and lay His hand upon people.
Please start today. It is the first an assignment and a commandment for us.
Pray for grace each time you go out for preaching and witnessing. Amen.
May the Lord bless you in Jesus name!

October 25

Good morning Father, Good morning Jesus, Good morning Holy Spirit.

Reading passage
John 20:19-21

Find your watch Word
John 20:20b (Memorise)

Prayer
Are you happy or glad when you are told about the things of the Lord, when you read the Gospel or when you are asked to come and work for God (kingdom service)?
The disciples were glad when they saw Jesus resurrected because that was their peace.
Your peace is carrying out your kingdom service, preaching the Gospel about Christ's resurrection and what He did in your life.
Pray for grace of God. Amen.
May the Lord bless you in Jesus name!

October 26

Good morning Father, Good morning Jesus, Good morning Holy Spirit.

Reading passage
James 3:2-5

Find your watch Word
James 3:5 (Memorise)

Prayer
The tongue is a deadly instrument; it can destroy and can bless – Joshua 1:8. Are you using your tongue to create life or to destroy life?
Learn not to use your tongue to destroy other people, use it to build up and not to cast down.
Do not use your tongue to gossip or backbite. God said we should declare a thing and it will be established. Do not use your tongue to declare negative to yourself or others so that negative is not established.
Choose to bless than curse yourself and/or others. Rise up in the morning and make good declarations about yourself and brethren.
It is well with you! Declare this morning things that are good and excellent over your life. Amen.
May the Lord bless you in Jesus name!

October 27

Good morning Father, Good morning Jesus, Good morning Holy Spirit.

Reading passage
Joshua 14:10-12

Find your watch Word
Joshua 14:11 (Memorise)

Prayer
The older you are in the Lord, the stronger you are. No age limit in the service of God. Caleb said in the reading of this morning (verse 11), my year is fourscore and five and I am as strong to go in and out to war.

In (verse 12) he said give me this mountain. What is the mountain you've requested the Lord to give you. Up till your old age, you can command your liberty and your deliverance.

Ask from the Lord to give you the desire of your age. Arise this morning and ask God to give to your hand that which belongs to you. Amen.

May the Lord bless you in Jesus name!

October 28

Good morning Father, Good morning Jesus, Good morning Holy Spirit.

Reading passage
Romans 8:27-28

Find your watch Word
Romans 8:28 (Memorise)

Prayer
God works for the good of those who love Him. Whatsoever happens in their life, He makes it to work out for their good.
God will never disappoint you when you are in pain, He is in pain, when you are happy, He is happy. So anything you are passing through now is not forever.
All you need to do is to trust God in your situation and hold to Him until your change comes.
Declare the Word of life and truth, hold to the Word God gives you during in your study time and prayers.
I assure you that all will work out for you to His glory. Amen.
May the Lord bless you in Jesus name!

October 29

Good morning Father, Good morning Jesus, Good morning Holy Spirit.

Reading passage
Ecclesiastes 3:12-14

Find your watch Word
Ecclesiastes 3:12 (Memorise)

Prayer
The preacher said there is nothing good for man but to rejoice and be happy. The good gift God gives to man and where he dwells Himself is happiness and rejoicing. It is good for man to rejoice in whatever situation he finds himself and then cry to God.
It is in rejoicing and not being depressed that God will answer man. He must not be mournful and downcast in his spirit.
My dear brother and sister, in your challenges and afflictions God will answer you.
Worship and praise God this morning and pray for His help. He will deliver you. Amen.
May the Lord bless you in Jesus name!

October 30

Good morning Father, Good morning Jesus, Good morning Holy Spirit.

Reading passage
John 16:13-15

Find your watch Word
John 16:14 (Memorise)

Prayer
Jesus Christ came to this world and returned to the Father and sat with God on the throne in heaven.
Exactly what He did He said the saints will do. But He (Jesus) left the Spirit to instruct us of what will come and what to do.
In verse 14 of our reading today, He said "He shall glorify me for he shall receive of mine, and show it unto you".
The Lord will enhance your understanding. Pray for the Holy Spirit to enlighten your eye of understanding today and instruct you on what to do. Amen.
May the Lord bless you in Jesus name!

October 31

Good morning Father, Good morning Jesus, Good morning Holy Spirit.

Reading passage
Matthew 13:26-28

Find your watch Word
Matthew 13:28 (Memorise)

Prayer
The Lord is the one to undo what the enemy has done. When man slept all the enemy does is to put poison into the life of man.
That is why the scripture says that the lukewarm and the unserious, God will spew out of His mouth – (Revelations 3:16-17).
Do not be lukewarm in your prayers but always be strong in prayers and always be a terror to the kingdom of darkness.
The enemy will not be able to touch you. Praise the Lord.
Do not allow the enemy to put any curse on you. Amen.
May the Lord bless you in Jesus name!

November 1

Good morning Father, Good morning Jesus, Good morning Holy Spirit.

Reading passage
Proverbs 16: 1-3

Find your watch Word
Proverbs 16:2 (Memorise)

Prayer
My beloved the Lord weighs your spirit and actions.
The scripture says guard your heart with all diligence for out of it are the issues of life. These issues of life can be evil imagination or good plans; it depends on which one you put on.
Kindly let your heart be for God's agenda always and not for any evil thoughts or plans. God sees the heart of men.
Let joy be your 'Find your watch Word'. Pray for the grace to maintain a state of heart that is right. God bless you. Amen.
May the Lord bless you in Jesus name!

November 2

Good morning Father, Good morning Jesus, Good morning Holy Spirit.

Reading passage
Psalms 36:5-9

Find your watch Word
Psalms 36:7b, 9b (Memorise)

Prayer
God is the trust that is surest. If you put your trust in Him, He will never let you down or disappoint you. He did not disappoint Shadrach, Meshach, Abednego and Daniel (Daniel 3:12) was not disappointed in the lion's den. Verse 9 of Psalms 36 says in the light of God, we shall see light. In the lesson of today "Trust" is very symbolic in the "light of God" (Verses 7b & 9b). The trust of God is in His light.
Pray for the grace to trust God is the light.
Hallelujah. Amen.
May the Lord bless you in Jesus name!

November 3

Good morning Father, Good morning Jesus, Good morning Holy Spirit.

Reading passage
Jeremiah 33: 6-8

Find your watch Word
Jeremiah 33: 6 (Memorise)

Prayer
The Lord has promised to give health and cure. Are you facing a time of illness and disease. God has declared the Good News you are requesting from Him.
Do not go about telling everyone that you have headache, stomach problem, etc. so that the angel of darkness will not establish it.
All Satan wants you to do is to announce your feelings, as soon as you start saying it to sister A or brother C, you discover the illness or disease will gain ground, contrary to the Gospel truth.
So keep your mouth shut and declare the word of God. He said He has given you health and cure. The physicians cannot cure, but the Lord said He gives you the cure.
That sickness and/or disease shall be terminated today and forever in Jesus name. Turn it to Him in prayer now. Amen.
May the Lord bless you in Jesus name!

November 4

Good morning Father, Good morning Jesus, Good morning Holy Spirit.

Reading passage
2 Corinthians 5:14-17

Find your watch Word
2 Corinthians 5:16 (Memorise)

Prayer
Jesus Christ died for us that we will not live for ourselves but live for God alone. In verse 17 of the reading passage for today, the scripture says, "he that live for Christ is a new creature, the old things have passed away but all things have become new".
Today you must check yourself to know if you are living for Christ or not. All things are now new in you including your thoughts, speech, eating, etc. Pray for God to renew you today and be fulfilled in the Lord. Amen.
May the Lord bless you in Jesus name!

November 5

Good morning Father, Good morning Jesus, Good morning Holy Spirit.

Reading passage
Romans 8:22-24

Find your watch Word
Romans 8:24 (Memorise)

Prayer
The scripture says that the hope that is seen is no longer hope. The hope that is seen need not be waited for. The hope in Christ Jesus needs patience.

The Spirit of God helps us during our waiting period. The scripture says the Spirit makes intercession for us.

Accept the Spirit of God today to help you, and make intercessions for you as you patiently wait in hope for God to perfect that which concerns you. Amen.

May the Lord bless you in Jesus name!

November 6

Good morning Father, Good morning Jesus, Good morning Holy Spirit.

Reading passage
Habakkuk 2:3-5

Find your watch Word
Habakkuk 3:4 (Memorise)

Prayer
The just shall live by their faith. Your faith should be lifted up for you to receive something tangible from the Lord.
If you meddle about with your faith, then your destiny is in danger.
Verse 4b says the just shall live by their faith. If your faith goes down, God will not pleased. Pray for God to empower and build your faith. Amen.
May the Lord bless you in Jesus name!

November 7

Good morning Father, Good morning Jesus, Good morning Holy Spirit.

Reading passage
James 5:20

Find your watch Word
James 5: 16b (Memorise)

Prayer

Is your prayer effectual? The Bible is referring to the prayer of Elias. His prayer was fervent and effectual. Your prayer life must be effective and consistent.

The scripture says, we shall declare a thing and it will be established. Let the earth know that you mean your declaration. This has to do with your faith.

May the Lord give you understanding to know that the Word of God says that as the rain comes to the earth and does not return until it wets the earth, so shall the Word accomplish its purpose. Pray today and mean your prayers.

November 8

Good morning Father, Good morning Jesus, Good morning Holy Spirit.

Reading passage
Psalms 113:5-9

Find your watch Word
Psalms 113:7 (Memorise)

Prayer
The Lord enthrones and dethrones. He humbled Himself to die on the Cross. He lifted the poor from the dunghill to sit with kings and princes. Always humble yourself in all situations.
He wants us to be humble and not be arrogant. Satan was proud and arrogant in heaven and he was cast out into the world.
Ask God to forgive you all your sins of arrogance and pride.
Then ask God for His infinite mercy. He is kind and merciful – (Isaiah 54:10b).
Pray that laziness shall not be resident in you.
Amen.
May the Lord bless you in Jesus name!

November 9

Good morning Father, Good morning Jesus, Good morning Holy Spirit.

Reading passage
Proverbs 12:17-19

Find your watch Word
Proverbs 12: 18 (Memorise)

Prayer
The tongue of the wise is health – (verse 18b). The wise knows what to say, and he handles his word with faith and assurance.
From the scripture, one can deduce that the wise is also righteous and pure.
Always make sure your ways are pure; be wise in all situations and call on God for help.
A wise man will always rest on God and call for His help. He is the only wise God.
Pray for the help of God to be wise. Amen.
May the Lord bless you in Jesus name!

November 10

Good morning Father, Good morning Jesus, Good morning Holy Spirit.

Reading passage
Mark 6:2-3

Find your watch Word
Mark 6:6 (Memorise)

Prayer
God is not happy about your unbelief. I do not know if you are part of those who call Jesus Christ the child of a carpenter.
Be careful not to accept any of Satan's interpretation and the twisting of God's word. Jesus Christ needed you to be saved and to decorate your life.
Only believe, do not join others to carelessly yield yourself to Satan to be used. I pray the Lord will give you understanding.
Pray that God will deliver you from the captivity of darkness.
You are loosed from the deceit of Satan in Jesus name. Amen.
May the Lord bless you in Jesus name!

November 11

Good morning Father, Good morning Jesus, Good morning Holy Spirit.

Reading passage
Proverbs 3:4-7

Find your watch Word
Proverbs 3:7 (Memories)

Prayer
We are only preserved by the special grace of God. It's not by our knowledge and understanding or wisdom. My brother and sister, be not wise in your own eyes. Trust in God and reference His love and greatness in your victories and life. The life of a man is not dependent on what he or she possesses.

Let your gratitude be made known to God in all you do. It is by His grace we sleep well and wake up, breathe, walk, acknowledge, hope, eat, drink, etc. Hallelujah!

When you go out or come in, give thanks to God. This morning reference the Lord upon your victories and joys. Just give Him thanks over your concerns. Amen.

May the Lord bless you in Jesus name!

November 12

Good morning Father, Good morning Jesus, Good morning Holy Spirit.

Reading passage
Job 22:26-29

Find your watch Word
Job 22:28 (Memorise)

Prayer
'You shall decree a thing and it shall come to pass". It shall be established in my name. What does it mean?
You shall say a thing and it shall be done. How do you decree?
It's by your prayer, by your word. Whatsoever you say with your mouth is a decree. What is a problem for you?
Is it to say a thing or to pray?
God will help your understanding. God is kind to us. He answers all our requests. You can be greedy spiritually, our Pastor told us.
So you can continue to decree in thousands and God will do it. Do not let Satan through fear rob you of your blessing. Open your mouth and decree today. Amen.
May the Lord bless you in Jesus name!

November 13

Good morning Father, Good morning Jesus, Good morning Holy Spirit.

Reading passage
Revelation 2:23-25

Find your watch Word
Revelation 2:25 (Memorise)

Prayer
The Lord has commanded us to hold on till He comes. Jesus Christ is coming again. All we have to do is to be prayerful and work the work of our Father. The kingdom service is very important and leading souls to Christ.

Go into the world and preach the Gospel. The Gospel of Christ is perfect. If we refuse to do this work, others will. There is no disappointment in the Lord.

The work of the kingdom is for us and our home. What service do you offer to the House of God? Do you go out often to preach the Word of God? Answer the question to yourself. Pray it out now. Amen.

May the Lord bless you in Jesus name!

November 14

Good morning Father, Good morning Jesus, Good morning Holy Spirit.

Reading passage
Proverbs 27:1-2

Find your watch Word
Proverbs 27:1 (Memorise)

Prayer
Do not boast of tomorrow but only boast in the Lord who is your anchor.
The scripture says even if I walk in the valley of death, I shall fear no evil – (Psalms 23:4). You have no power of your own. Jesus Christ said that why do you want to boast of yourself.
Rest on God in all your situations. He will deliver you. He is always with us.
The water of the earth will not overtake us. Jesus is Lord. Amen.
May the Lord bless you in Jesus name!

November 15

Good morning Father, Good morning, good morning Holy Spirit.

Reading passage
Proverbs 21:6-8

Find your watch Word
Proverbs 21:6 (Memorise)

Prayer
The Word of the Lord in Romans 6:23 says the soul that sins shall die. God does not joke with His commandments.

As a child of God, you are not allowed to lie or walk in sin. Always remember the soul that sins shall die. God is no respecter of any man and He does not play with His covenant.

The Bible says God exalts His Word above His name. So if that is in the scripture, imagine what is going to happen to any sinner.

Go on your knees right now and ask God for the forgiveness of your sins. God help you and have mercy on you. Amen.

May the Lord bless you in Jesus name!

November 16

Good morning Father, Good morning Jesus, Good morning Holy Spirit.

Reading passage
Proverbs 3:27-28

Find your watch Word
1 John 3:17 (Memorise)

Prayer
The word of God says you must not shut your door when your brother or sister is in need of something that you have.
Do you tell your friend I do not know how many times you have said no to your friend, stop and change your way of life today and share with your sister and brother both in Christ and those who are not?
Give and it shall be given to you. Giving increases you, it does not reduce you. Do not tell him or her that asks you to give them to go and come back later except it's a thing of sin – (Proverbs 3:27-28).
Pray that God will forgive you and start a new life of giving and sharing today. Amen.
May the Lord bless you in Jesus name!

November 17

Good morning Father, Good morning Jesus, Good morning Holy Spirit.

Reading passage
2 Corinthians 4:6-8

Find your watch Word
2 Corinthians 4:8 (Memorise)

Prayer
The Lord is our defence. No matter what the trouble you are passing through the Lord is faithful, He will strengthen and empower you. You will not be distressed, God will guide your going out and coming in.

Do not be perplexed or despair. God has a special cover for us when we pass through tribulation or afflictions and trials. He keeps His word, "I will never leave you nor forsake you"- (Hebrew 13:5b).

Though, sometimes we believe not that God abides faithful – (2 Timothy 2:13), keep yourself in His peace, relax in the hands of God and He will glorify Himself in you. You will not be put to shame. Amen.

May the Lord bless you in Jesus name!

November 18

Good morning Father, Good morning Jesus, Good morning Holy Spirit.

Reading passage
Judges 6:7-12

Find your watch Word
Judges 6:10-12 (Memorise)

Prayer
The Lord is a deliverer but we need to speak to Him and cried our heart to Him and trust in Him without doubt – James 1:8. A double minded person does not receive from the Lord. When you give anything to God, you need not go and ask Him whether it is safe or not. God is greater than your parents. If you ask your Mum to buy you your uniform you do not go back to her before she buys it. She was not deaf. God forgive us anyhow. So when you have spoken about your need to Him, start to praise Him and give thanks to Him without any doubt our desire will come. If you have asked God to do something then start to give Him thanks. He will bring a living proof to you.
Amen.
May the Lord bless you in Jesus name!

November 19

Good morning Father, Good morning Jesus, Good morning Holy Spirit.

Reading passage
Psalms 37:4-5

Find your watch Word
Psalms 37:5 (Memorise)

Prayer

The Lord wants us to handover all our situations for Him to handle. He wants to expand us, multiply us and increase us – Jeremiah 30:19b. We children of God like to live a life of littleness. That is, we are satisfied with the small that we have. Do not hold to smallness always but give God a place in your life to increase you more and more.

If you passed level or Year 9 examinations go for another one that is higher than that. Everything they said is difficult, go for it with the Spirit and mind of Christ in you.

This makes you to know better of God and what God can do in your life. With this you preach the Gospel to other with your life and steps.

Pray that God will enlarge your insight and inspiration about what God can do. "More exceeding abundantly". Amen.

May the Lord bless you in Jesus name!

November 20

Good morning Father, Good morning Jesus, Good morning Holy Spirit.

Reading passage
Psalms 132:4-5

Find your watch Word
Psalm 130:6 (Memorise)

Prayer
Those that watch for the morning are called a security, which means they do not sleep at night when others are sleeping in their bed.
Are you waiting for God at all? How will God put you in the first place in His book of remembrance? Psalms 132:4 says that God will neither slumber nor sleep.
The kingdom of God is work; you have to desire it before you can have it.
You read for your examination before you can pass. I mean good pass. God will help you.
Whatever is good does not come cheap or free.
When they announce the night vigil do not stay at home and sleep.
Search for the Lord and you will find Him. Pray for special grace. Amen.
May the Lord bless you in Jesus name!

November 21

Good morning Father, Good morning Jesus, Good morning Holy Spirit.

Reading passage
Psalms 37:1-2

Find your watch Word
Psalms 37:29 (Memorise)

Prayer
The righteous may pass through difficult times but if he can wait for God, he will definitely rejoice – Jeremiah 1:19. They will surely fight but will not prevail. Who has passed through the time they call hard time. Time changes, man changes, but God will never change.

When the fight becomes turf that is the time you should hold on and stand. Something good is on the way for you because the righteous is destined to inherit the land.

Do not look at what that your friend is wearing or the type of car he's riding. Endure the hard time because the unbeliever does not last with their master. The devil has a definite time he will always destroy his people. The devil does not have any good gift.

Pray today for the grace to carry through the time of trial – (John 17:14). Amen.

May the Lord bless you in Jesus name!

November 22

Good morning Father, Good morning Jesus, Good morning Holy Spirit.

Reading passage
Matthew 6:19-20

Find your watch Word
Malachi 3:10 (Memorise)

Prayer
The Lord commanded us to pay our tithe in our Find your watch Word for today. This is an insurance that covers our life and destiny from destruction by the devil. You might not be working but you are either blessed by your parents or friends.

Children learn to pay your tithe from even your upkeep given to you by your parents either weekly or monthly. Tithe should be taken from any increase in your life.

The 10% of any increase called tithe is a treasure in heaven not only on earth. This includes your offering, vows and other sacrifices. Your house will not be empty in heaven.

Make a covenant of payment of all your treasures today and watch your recovery. Satan will not swallow up your destiny because of disobedience in Jesus name. Amen.

May the Lord bless you in Jesus name!

November 23

Good morning Father, Good morning Jesus, Good morning Holy Spirit.

Reading passage
John 16:14-16

Find your watch Word
John 16:15 (Memorise)

Prayer
Jesus Christ is making it known to us the importance of the Spirit of God called the Comforter. If you look at verse 15 of the passage, the Lord Jesus said all that the Father has belongs to Him.

If you are a joint heir with Christ, you have all that the Father has. So you have the right of inheritance to claim all.

I pray that your eye of understanding will be opened to know all that has been freely given to you in Christ. Amen.

May the Lord bless you in Jesus name!

November 24

Good morning Father, Good morning Jesus, Good morning Holy Spirit.

Reading passage
Psalms 44:1-8

Find your watch Word
Psalms 44:6 (Memorise)

Prayer
My dear reader by yourself you can do nothing. Look unto God who is able to help you. Give all to Him, let God know you actually give all to Him when He searches your heart.
Psalms 44:8 says in God we boast. Can you boast in the Lord?
The Israelite in verse 3 of this passage says they did not possess the land by their sword.
What are you thinking you can do by yourself today?
Leave it to God, He will help you.
Pray for His help and open up yourself to God. Take time to study the scripture and listen to His voice. He is your HELP. Amen.
May the Lord bless you in Jesus name!

November 25

Good morning Father, Good morning Jesus, Good morning Holy Spirit.

Reading passage
Psalms 37:37-40

Find your watch Word
Psalms 37:39 (Memorise)

Prayer
The wicked cannot by any means take the place of the righteous. God is always upset with the wicked every day. The wicked cannot miss the judgement of the Lord. I want you to be at peace and trust God with all your heart. God is ready to take vengeance on all that troubles you.
The reading passage verse 39 said the Lord is your strength in times of trouble. Verse 40b of today's reading passage says the Lord will save the righteous because they trust in Him. Trust in the Lord and serve the Lord, you will see the act of God to those who rest on Him.
Pray that God should stabilise you in His peace so that you will completely rest in Him and wait to see His salvation. Amen.
May the Lord bless you in Jesus name!

November 26

Good morning Father, Good morning Jesus, Good morning Holy Spirit.

Reading passage
Luke 19:21-22

Find your watch Word
Luke 19:21 (Memorise)

Prayer
Do not allow fear stop your deliverance. Any influence of fear is a hindrance. It rubs you of your confidence to go forward.
"Do not fear" appears in the scripture more than 365 times to cover each day of the year. So each day has its own 'do not be afraid'.
Jesus said to the disciples do not be afraid. I know some times the fear will come to try you, but the only way for you to overcome is to relax in the hand of God.
The three Hebrew men (Meshach, Shadrach aand Abednego) said if it is death, so be it than to bow to your golden image, O king.
The Lord sent Jesus into the burning furnace before they got there. They came out alive. Amen.
May the Lord bless you in Jesus name!

November 27

Good morning Father, Good morning Jesus, Good morning Holy Spirit.

Reading passage
Philippians 3:15-18

Find your watch Word
Philippians 3:16 (Memorise)

Prayer
Whatsoever we have been taught, we should strive to walk in them. It's very important to walk in what we have attained because Satan the accuser of the brethren is watching us every day. Our salvation is not permanent until we die and go to heaven.

It's a day to day process. So if we are found unfaithful, we can lose our salvation if we are not careful. Satan does not sleep but always looks for means to bring us back to the ways of the world. Let us stand firm in the doctrine of God and watch every day. God will uphold you to the end. Today, ask the Lord to help you to be consistent in your standing before Him and fervent too. Amen. May the Lord bless you in Jesus name!

November 28

Good morning Father, Good morning Jesus, Good morning Holy Spirit.

Reading passage
Jeremiah 29:8-11

Find your watch Word
Jeremiah 29:11 (Memorise)

Prayer
God has a plan for everyone because any child of God is a joint heir with Christ. When we become joint heirs with Christ, God thinks about us and has His plans ready for each one of us. For you to know that what I just said is true, you must always be fervent with God.
Read the His word always and think about His Kingdom. The thoughts of good that God has for you will definitely come to pass.
On the other hand, if you are negligent of God, His word and His kingdom, you may not be able to discover this plan that God has for you. Good will attend your way when you acquaint yourself with God, the King of kings – (Job 22:21). Amen.
May the Lord bless you in Jesus name!

November 29

Good morning Father, Good morning Jesus, Good morning Holy Spirit.

Reading Passage
Proverbs 4: 23-24

Find your watch word
Proverbs 4: 23-24 (Memorise)

Prayer
Guard your heart from the spirit of unbelief. Always be careful with your heart. God does not want anybody to interact with or come to Him in unbelief.

Many of the children of Israel died in the wilderness because unbelief. Jesus Christ recognised that the unbelieving can believe what the Lord has in store for them.

The first thing they need to do is believe God's Word and His commandment; that is what moves the hand of God to act on your behalf.

Pray for the heart to believe God and His word today. You shall surely see the glory of the Lord. Out of your heart is the well spring of life. Amen. May the Lord bless you in Jesus name!

November 30

Good morning Father, Good morning Jesus, Good morning Holy Spirit.

Reading passage
Psalms 35:10-12

Find your watch Word
Psalms 35:10 (Memorise)

Prayer
There are some situations that come to test of your faith. It may be so intense to the extent that you may want to ask God what is happening. Jesus Christ on the cross of Calvary said "My Father if this can be removed from me, but let thy will be done". God knows there are situations that can become unbearable but still He wants us to trust Him. Psalms 35:10 says "all my bones shall say who is like unto thee".......... the word is based on trust. It was all the bones of this man that is to trust God. The bones of his body, including the marrows. Put your trust in God, He is a powerful deliverer. Problems are real, afflictions are real but the deliverance of Jesus Christ from all of them is more real.
Pray today and trust the Lord that is able to deliver. Enjoy your freedom through the blood of Jesus Christ. Jesus is Lord. Amen.
May the Lord bless you in Jesus name!

December 1

Good morning Father, Good morning Jesus, Good morning Holy Spirit.

Reading passage
Psalms 119:142-144

Find your watch Word
Psalms 119:144 (Memorise)

Prayer
The testimony of God is in His Word, but the understanding of the Word is called testimony because it brings testimonies to you.
The very Find your watch Word of today says give me understanding and I shall live. Without understanding of the word of God, there can be no life. You need to pray yourself out of ignorance today and your eye of understanding will be opened for you to experience and enjoy the testimony of God to live.
The word of God is the only thing that can set you free. So desire the deliverance through the word of God today to live an enviable life. Amen.
May the Lord bless you in Jesus name!

December 2

Good morning Father, Good morning Jesus, Good morning Holy Spirit.

Reading passage
Exodus 23:25-26

Find your watch Word
Exodus 23:25 (Memorise)

Prayer
The service of the Lord is His delight. You need to serve the Lord to move God. The only thing that moves the hands of God to fight on your behalf is service in His kingdom and walking in line with His word – (1 Thessalonians 4:3).

Our hearts must be sanctified to go in line with the word of God. Anybody who only professes with his or her mouth without walking in line with the word of God is deceiving himself.

God says, He exalts His word more than His name. What God will not do, He will not say. He is not a man. The Lord moves by the understanding of His word in every man. When you serve Him, His promise is to bless all that you have – (verse 25). You will not suffer lack and want.

You will not die prematurely. It is true but you must serve and believe that this word, and you will experience it. Think about it! Amen.

May the Lord bless you in Jesus name!

December 3

Good morning Father, Good morning Jesus, Good morning Holy Spirit.

Reading passage
Proverbs 20:27-28

Find your watch Word
Proverb 20:27 (Memorise)

Prayer
The Spirit of man is the candle of the Lord that searches the heart. When the spirit of man interacts with the word of God, it does a lot of things through the Holy Spirit. Let the word of God rule your spirit, soul and body.
This is the access for you to rule your world. Verse 26 of the passage is anchored by the scripture that says "mercy and truth preserves the King". You are a king – (Psalms 82:6).
When you give your life to Christ, even the evil spirit from the pit of hell knows.
The scripture says we are transformed from darkness into light.
Pray for grace to live a life of great understanding of who the Lord is. God bless you. Amen.
May the Lord bless you in Jesus name!

December 4

Good morning Father, Good morning Jesus, Good morning Holy Spirit.

Reading passage
1 John 4:7-8

Find your watch Word
1 John 4:8 (Memorise)

Prayer
The birth of Jesus Christ portrays the love of God to us. If Jesus was not born, we would have been in the boat of the evil one called Satan; but the birth of Jesus took us out of destruction.
This you will understand, if you think of what king Herod wanted to do to Jesus after He was born.
They planned to kill Him knowing His mission of deliverance. Child of God, if we do not love God and our neighbours, we are visitors in the kingdom. I pray that God give us a real understanding of today's scripture.
Ask for forgiveness, rededicate your life and start a new life of love today. It is well with you. Amen.
May the Lord bless you in Jesus name!

December 5

Good morning Father, Good morning Jesus, Good morning Holy Spirt.

Reading passage
Romans 5:8-10

Find your watch Word
Romans 5:10 (Memorise)

Prayer
Jesus Christ is the Lamb of God that was slaughtered for the remission of our sin. God only made His love available for us with the crucifixion of Jesus Christ.
When Jesus was born there was problem in the spirit world. God kept His detailed plan about Jesus Christ secret until the time was right for the plan of God for man to be fulfilled.
The Blood of Jesus Christ paid it all. We must have protection from God. Amen.
May the Lord bless you in Jesus name!

December 6

Good morning Father, Good morning Jesus, Good morning Holy Spirit.

Reading passage
Psalms 18:27-29

Find your watch Word
Psalms 18:28 (Memorise)

Prayer
The Scripture says God will save His people from afflicted people and bring down His look – (Psalms 18:27).
Everything that is high look in our lives such as sicknesses, lack, stagnation, poverty, failure, etc. God promised to bring them down. God will enlighten our darkness – (Psalms 18:28).
Children of light must not live in darkness. God Himself is light unto us. Let us carry this mentality and believe God can help us.
If God does not help us no man can. I declare today every darkness around us be turned to light. Jesus Christ was sent to enlighten our darkness.
The Christmas season is a season of light because the "Light" is born in the person of Jesus Christ. Our light will shine forth from now into the new year in Jesus name. Amen.
May the Lord bless you in Jesus name!

December 7

Good morning Father, Good morning Jesus, Good morning Holy Spirit.

Reading passage
John 6:1-11

Find your watch Word
John 6:11 (Memorise)

Prayer
Jesus is a role model for all of His children. In the reading passage for this morning, Jesus showed Himself as a meek and humble steward. In verse 6 of the reading passage Jesus asked the disciples what they think they can give to the people to eat. Jesus gave them the opportunity to speak out their own idea.
He was neither selfish nor proud, even though He is God. Jesus knew He could provide it but considered others first. Do you normally do that? Learn from the Master. In verse 11, Jesus gave thanks. Children of God should always learn to give thanks in all things. Jesus is our example. Not proud, not selfish, not greedy of anything or in anything. God will always teach you. Learn, learn child of God from the Master.
Pray for the Spirit of humility, meekness and gentleness. Give thanks for this month of Christmas.
Amen.
May the Lord bless you in Jesus name!

December 8

Good morning Father, Good morning Jesus, Good morning Holy Spirit.

Reading passage
Psalms 112:7-9

Find your watch Word
Psalms 112:8 (Memorise)

Prayer
Is your heart established in the Lord? Do you feel immoveable in the kingdom? All you need to do is to make yourself a mountain that cannot be moved by fellowshipping with God.
Put the word of God in your heart and ensure that souls are saved for the extension of His kingdom. This is how you can be established in the kingdom. Do not allow Satan to push you in and out. Your foundation is in Christ. Love others as yourself. The law of love is very important for you. Amen.
May the Lord bless you in Jesus name!

December 9

Good morning Father, Good morning Jesus, Good morning Holy Spirit.

Reading passage
Job 29:3-5

Find your watch Word
Job 29:4 (Memorise)

Prayer
Remember the Lord in the days of your youth when the evil day is not yet come – (Ecclesiastes 12:1).
My brothers and sisters, Job did mention the day of his youth which means the Lord had being with him in his youthful time.
This is the time for you to move closer to God and remember Jesus is the Vine and you are the branch of Him. Verse 4 of Job 29 says '... I was in the days of my youth, the secret of God was upon my tabernacle'. The secret of God was with Job from his youth. Now is the time God wants to reveal the secret of His kingdom to you. Make a room for the Lord in your life, heart, soul and body. God loves you as a child, as a youth, and also as an adult. Your answer with God should be speedy and straight forward. What do you wish to do today? "BE ESTABLISHED IN Christ Jesus". Take a decision. Go to God in prayer. Amen.
May the Lord bless you in Jesus name!

December 10

Good morning Father, Good morning Jesus, Good morning Holy Spirit.

Reading passage
Philippians 4:8-9

Find your watch Word
Philippians 4:8 (Memorise)

Prayer
This reading passage today talks about all things that are expected of a child of God. They are really the fruit of a genuine child of God. I mean born again child of God.
These are the fruit you should bear. Try as much as possible to write out these fruits. Are you sure you are after the kingdom?
Then pen these fruits on paper as in verse 8 of Philippians chapter 4.
Hang the paper on the wall in your house where you can easily see it everyday, to see how you have lived up to the fruits each day.
Pray for the grace of God. Amen.
May the Lord bless you in Jesus name!

December 11

Good morning Father, Good morning Jesus, Good morning Holy Spirit.

Reading passage
Psalms 34:4-5, & 19-20

Find your watch Word
Psalms 34: 4-5 (Memorise)

Prayer
The word of the Lord says they looked unto God, they were radiant. Who are the they? "Saints" like you, the child of the living God.

The scripture says in verse 4b, "I sought the Lord and He heard me". Have you ever sought the Lord? I mean in prayers?. You look for a quiet place to seek Him, not a noisy area. Verse 19-20 says He kept him none of his bones were broken. God can keep you.

This month is the last month of the year, what are you still looking for? "Seek Him" the year has not ended yet. Do you even have a list of things you are believing God for in the coming year? TRUST THE LORD, you will not regret it, your face will not be put to shame.

Wait on the Lord. Pray for the grace to look, seek and trust in Jesus. He gives freely. Amen.
May the Lord bless you in Jesus name!

December 12

Good morning Father, Good morning Jesus, Good morning Holy Spirit.

Reading passage
Psalms 92:13

Find your watch Word
Psalms 92:13b (Memorise)

Prayer
This year is the year you will flourish in the court of the Lord. Declare this verse 13b and make sure you use it to pray this morning. As you go out everything that had run dry in your life, shall rise and start to flourish – Ezekiel 37:3,5.

You shall receive fresh breath from the Lord today, the breath to flourish. Start to flourish from today in Jesus name.

I have a feeling that God wants you to hold tightly to this scripture in your declaration and prayer until you receive something tangible from Him.
Amen.
May the Lord bless you in Jesus name!

December 13

Good morning Father, Good morning Jesus, Good morning Holy Spirit.

Reading passage
Proverbs 3:9-10

Find your watch Word
Proverbs 3:9 (Memorise)

Prayer

You need to pray fervently for the grace to give. Giving to man and mostly to God is very important for divine blessing.

Blessing does not only mean finance but health and the meeting of every other necessity. The scripture is asking you to give to God the increase of all your first fruits. It actually involves anything that increases in your life. Honour the Lord the Giver, do not leave the Giver and exalt the gift. Blessing stays where it's being used for its purpose. God command blessing and can command curse. God will enlighten your understanding.

It's time for us to know our purpose; the scripture calls us the salt of the earth. This means we are meant to put sweetness into the life of many, where sweetness is lacking. I pray that your substance and your own source of blessing will not seize in Jesus name.

Pray for this grace of ceaseless blessing and giving.
Amen.
May the Lord bless you in Jesus name!

December 14

Good morning, Good morning Jesus, Good morning Holy Spirit.

Reading passage
Isaiah 1:19-20

Find your watch Word
Isaiah 1:19 (Memorise)

Prayer
The Lord is a Father who wants us to be obedient in all that concerns spiritual leadings. The power of God will always work for us as and when we obey.

Willingness to obey is a treasure but Satan also knows the blessings attached to obedience, so he goes all the way to block the path of obedience of the children of Light (God).

You have to be sensitive to all God's commandments. Sometimes Satan uses man (friends, colleagues, family) to hinder our way of obedience so that our blessings may be blocked or obstructed. Think before you yield to any human advice. God will grant you insight in decision making.

Pray for this grace to overcome all satanic techniques to block your blessings. Amen.
May the Lord bless you in Jesus name!

December 15

Good morning Father, Good morning Jesus, Good morning Holy Spirit.

Reading passage
2 Corinthians 8:9; Proverbs 23:26

Find your watch Word
Proverbs 23:26 (Memorise)

Prayer
Put your heart and focus on the things that concern God and His Kingdom. God is very concerned about the advancement of His Kingdom. God wants to see souls saved.
If you can devout your time to the preaching of the Gospel, you will see the Lord on your side all the time.
As this year comes to end, count by yourself how many souls that have been saved through you or that you have preached the Gospel to.
What are all the things God is laying upon your heart for souls to be saved in the New Year? How many lives are you looking forward to touch? Lift up your voice and pray for those people. Amen.
May the Lord bless you in Jesus name!

December 16

Good morning Father, Good morning Jesus, Good morning Holy Spirit.

Reading passage
Proverbs 16:24-25

Find your watch Word
Proverbs 16:24 (Memorise)

Prayer
Pleasant words come out from the mouth of the wise. A child of God must always be slow to speak in any situation. We are the book that the world reads. Our words can be used by the world to judge us.

Whatever comes out of our mouth actually describe who we are. Jesus Christ is a good example of how we should behave or respond to situations.

Jesus will keep quiet for a while before He responds to anything said to Him by the Pharisees, the Sadducees and the Scribes. Learn to let the Heaven tell you what to say before you speak. Amen.

May the Lord bless you in Jesus name!

December 17

Good morning Father, Good morning Jesus, Good morning Holy Spirit.

Reading passage
2 Timothy 2:19-20

Find your watch Word
2 Timothy 2:19b (Memorise)

Prayer
It is a command for a child of God to depart from evil. If we do not depart from sin, it can kill. Write on a sheet of paper and paste on the wall in your room that 'sin is a killer; depart from it'. This will remind you all the time and help you to keep away from sin at all times.
God is preparing you for what He has in store for you. Be sure to let your generation must know that you live for Christ.
Desire it, go after it and ask for help to achieve it. God bless you. Amen.
May the Lord bless you in Jesus name!

December 18

Good morning Father, Good morning Jesus, Good morning Holy Spirit.

Reading passage
Psalms 16:10-11

Find your watch Word
Psalms 16:10 (Memorise)

Prayer
The Lord will not suffer you to see corruption. Do you believe this? The Lord said "I will never leave you nor forsake you".

God is in control of your life. What are you going through at the moment? God is able. Stand with God in prayer. Make sure you listen to God at all time.

You are the solution to your life. Sort yourself out with the Word of God and wait patiently. If there is anything you don't understand, please get counsel from the Pastor for rightful leading.

Pray for divine grace to make your way up in your youthful time – (Ecclesiastes 12:1). God bless you. Amen.

May the Lord bless you in Jesus name!

December 19

Good morning Father, Good morning Jesus, Good morning Holy Spirit.

Reading passage
2 Thessalonians 3:10b-11

Find your watch Word
2 Thessalonians 3:10b (Memorise)

Prayer
Let none of you be less busy in the house of the Lord. Satan creates job for whoever doesn't have job. Ensure you have something doing always. This is in the kingdom service as well as your secular work for living.

The scripture says that "he who does not work, should not eat". Verse 11 of the scripture of study today says they that do not work eventually become busy-bodies; they suspect others in the church, backbiting and strifing.

Keep yourself busy all the time and turn to God for direction.

Pray and receive grace for this task in Jesus name. Amen.

May the Lord bless you in Jesus name!

December 20

Good morning Father, Good morning Jesus, Good morning Holy Spirit.

Reading passage
John 15:5-7, 10

Find your watch Word
John 15:5b (Memorise)

Prayer
In this passage, the Lord Jesus Christ tells us the relationship between Himself and ourselves. Only He (Jesus) will be able to change our lives. The scripture in verse 5b says by yourself you can do nothing.

It's always good for God to help us because He does not waste our time, money, efforts, substance and whatever we have. If we wait on God, He will give us all that we do not have. See what verse 10 says, "If you keep my commandments", that is to say that our keeping His commandments matters.

Why? Because it's the requirement for verses 6 & 7 to happen. May the Lord give us understanding, Amen.

May the Lord bless you in Jesus name!

December 21

Good morning Father, Good morning Jesus, Good morning Holy Spirit.

Reading passage
Psalms 62:7-8

Find your watch Word
Psalms 62:8 (Memorise)

Prayer
In God is your refuge and deliverance so put your trust in Him. You might not have got the word raw like I am telling you. Do not make a mistake in life before you return to God.
It is good that you know God in your youthful or childhood age. He is the helper of man's life. Tell Him all about your life and trust your life into His hand. Take time to serve the Lord in the beauty of His holiness and in His house. He will reveal to you what you need to know.
Take His word with seriousness, He will lead you and send those who will help you on your way in life. Rest on God's hands; He will carry you through your life. Pray for God's help today.
Amen.
May the Lord bless you in Jesus name!

December 22

Good morning Father, Good morning Jesus, Good morning Holy Spirit.

Reading passage
Psalms 30:6-7

Find your watch Word
Psalms 30:7 (Memorise)

Prayer
The favour of God is the strength of His children. God is the Force behind our outstanding performance and advancement. He needs to be served with our might.
Take time to meditate on the word of God for today. We need the favour of God to prosper and to succeed in life.
I want you to praise the Lord for all His favour upon your life including that of your family. It is well with you and you are highly blessed and favoured. Amen.
May the Lord bless you in Jesus name!

December 23

Good morning Father, Good morning Jesus, Good morning Holy Spirit.

Reading Passage
Psalms 34:15-17

Find your watch Word
Psalms 34:15 (Memorise)

Prayer
The Lord knows those that are His. Everyone who names the name of the Lord should depart from evil. The Lord only listens to the prayer of the righteous (Psalms 34:15).
Who are the righteous? They are people with the heart for God; and who love God and their neighbours, and trust in the Lord at all times. Without faith nobody can see God. The verse 16 of our reading passage says 'the eyes of the Lord are against the evil one'.
We should live our lives to please God, because the scripture says in Luke 2:14, '... peace, goodwill towards men'. You have total peace, you must please the Lord. How? By total obedience to the commandment of God and complete trust in Him alone.
In your prayer this morning ask the Lord to give you the grace to have the heart for God in all that you do. Amen.
May the Lord bless you in Jesus name!

December 24

Good morning Father, Good morning Jesus, Good morning Holy Spirit.

Reading Passage
Psalms 92:14-15; Romans 8:38

Find your watch Word
Psalms 92:14 (Memorise)

Prayer
We should always be grateful to God in all things; there is nothing good without God. God is good and good is God. When we don't even have hope God stretches His hand of love towards us – Job 27:3. It's by the grace of God that you are breathing.

The year is coming to an end; think of the ways to give thanks to the Lord for all He has done for you in the year.

Every wondrous acts of God in your life is down to Him – (Psalms 67:5-7).

Count your blessings today and return to God in gratitude; and in anticipation for His multiple blessings for the coming year.

Go to God in prayer of gratitude. Amen.
May the Lord bless you in Jesus name!

December 25

Good morning Father, Good morning Jesus, Good morning Holy Spirit.

Reading Passage
Psalms 50:14-16

Find your watch Word
Psalms 50:14 (Memorise)

Prayer
MERRY CHRISTMAS, AND BEST WISHES FOR THE NEW YEAR! The Lord wants your heart of praise, so today I want you to give God your high praise. How do you give Him your high praise? Sit down for five minutes, take account of what He has done for you the whole of this year and thank Him that you are still alive till this day. Forget about all those things that He has not done for you.

In the early years there was a man who didn't give thanks to God, because he only had one pair of shoes. But soon after he saw a man without any legs in a wheel chair still giving thanks to God, and he regretted ever murmuring against God. So this morning stop murmuring and praise God any how. 'God has no beginning and no end' – (1 Corinthians 10:10). Amen.

May the Lord bless you in Jesus name!

December 26

Good morning Father, Good morning Jesus, Good morning Holy Spirit.

Reading Passage
Psalms 48:8-10

Find your watch Word
Psalms 48:9 (Memorise)

Prayer
The prayer of thanksgiving is very necessary at this particular time of the year. God is mighty and He has done wondrous things in His Church this year. I want you to thank God for His move this year in His kingdom, and in His Church. Thank God on behalf of all the ministers of God throughout the year.
Return to God all the praise. Amen.
May the Lord bless you in Jesus name!

December 27

Good morning Father, Good morning Jesus, Good morning Holy Spirit.

Reading Passage
Jeremiah 17:10,12

Find your watch Word
Jeremiah 17:10,12 (Memorise)

Prayer
The life of pride doesn't see anything to praise God for. Consider the book of Jeremiah 17 verse 10. God was speaking as the builder of the universe. In verse 12, He said He is the hope of Israel even your hope.
You consider yourself, do you have any other hope. It's by God's grace that you are not destroyed in the year that is ebbing out. Take about 30 minutes to praise and dance to God. Start to ask God for new things in the coming year.
Tell God to be your hope in the new year. Amen. May the Lord bless you in Jesus name!

December 28

Good morning Father, Good morning Jesus, Good morning Holy Spirit.

Reading Passage
Luke 1:43-45

Find your watch Word
Luke 1:45 (Memorise)

Prayer
There is always the performance of that, which the mouth of God has spoken. Do you take the word of God seriously when you read the scripture? Taste and see that the Lord is good. Every word of God in the Bible is powerful. The book of Job 32:8 says the spirit in the word of God gives inspiration and understanding. When you receive the word of God towards anything you are passing through, you must believe there shall be a "performance" of the word, therefore hold tenaciously to it.

You will be surprised the word will take you out of your bondage. Are you in a situation that looks difficult this day? Pray and wait on God; study the scripture to receive a word. There shall be a "PERFORMANCE". Amen.
May the Lord bless you in Jesus name!

December 29

Good morning Father, Good morning Jesus, Good morning Holy Spirit.

Reading Passage
Galatians 6:9-10

Find your watch Word
Galatians 6:10 (Memorise)

Prayer
It is always an opportunity when you meet with somebody you can help. The scripture says if there is a good thing you can do to someone, take the opportunity to quickly do it.
Why? This is because God always has alternative or a substitute. He will choose another person whom He will want to bless to do it.
There is a testimony of a man in my church, who chose to clean the house of God. But sometimes by the time he finished, there would be no one to take him home. He said to himself, "I will just wait and do this work". Most at times he walks to the station after the work. Later that same week God sent somebody to him, who gave him a car. Verse 10 is very inspiring, read it well and pray on it. Take it as a service and do well to all. Amen.
May the Lord bless you in Jesus name!

December 30

Good morning Father, Good morning Jesus, Good morning Holy Spirit.

Reading Passage
Proverbs 13:2-3

Find your watch Word
Proverbs 13:2 (Memorise)

Prayer
What do you say to yourself with your mouth? The scripture tells how the word of your mouth builds your purpose.

Watch what you say, your mouth is what determines your destiny. The tongue is a very powerful weapon which can be used for a good purpose, but it is also capable of a bad purpose. Sometimes people say things that they don't really mean, such as "I'm so stupid to have got that wrong".

This day I want you to pray against careless talk.
Amen.
May the Lord bless you in Jesus name!

December 31

Good morning Father, Good morning Jesus, Good morning Holy Spirit.

Reading Passage
Psalms 84:7-8

Find your watch Word
Psalms 84:7 (Memorise)

Prayer
They go from strength to strength every one of them in Zion. This tells you that those who go to Zion to serve God can only go from strength to strength.
If you do not go to church which the Bible refers to as Zion, I encourage you to think about it as you cross into the New Year.
There are a lot of packages in Zion where the Lord dwells. God bless you and have a Happy New Year! Amen.
May the Lord bless you in Jesus name!